CONFLICT IN THE
MIDDLE EAST
ISRAEL AN...

CONTENTS   i

Key Issue

- What was the Jewish claim to Palestine?

In 1948 the state of Israel was created out of the land of Palestine. Since then there has been almost continuous conflict between Israel and its Arab neighbours. The Middle East has hardly ever been out of the news. Why is this such a live issue? Whose land is it anyway? This chapter will examine the Jewish claim to Palestine.

THE EXPULSION OF THE JEWS FROM PALESTINE

From about 1500 BC, the Jewish people lived in the land of Palestine. In the time of Jesus – first century AD – Palestine was ruled by the Romans. In AD 70 and again in AD 135 the Jews rebelled against their Roman rulers. Roman soldiers crushed both revolts, destroyed the city of Jerusalem and expelled the Jews. Many thousands fled to neighbouring countries and, over the next 200 years, they settled in almost every part of the Roman Empire. Many became merchants and farmers, bankers and craftsmen. Some became wealthy and even gained important positions in the governments of the new lands in which they lived.

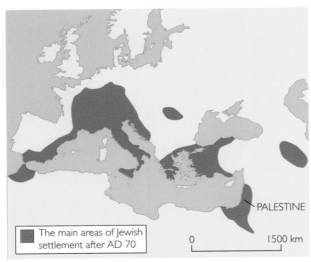

The main areas of Jewish settlement after AD 70

PALESTINE

0   1500 km

This map shows the main areas of Jewish settlement from AD 70 to the Middle Ages.

ANTI-SEMITISM IN EUROPE

Then, in the Middle Ages, the Jews were expelled from much of western Europe and many settled in Russia and Poland. But they were often **persecuted**. Almost all Europeans were Christians and they often forced the Jews to live in separate areas. The Jews were not allowed to vote or even to buy their own land. Such anti-Jewish behaviour is known as **anti-Semitism**.

In the nineteenth century, the country with the largest Jewish population was Russia. When the tsar, or emperor, was assassinated in 1881, there were many anti-Jewish riots. The new tsar's government encouraged the persecution of the Jews. **Synagogues** were burnt down, Jewish homes were attacked and thousands of Jews were killed. Many Russian Jews fled to western Europe and the USA. But, even there, Jews often found that they were not treated as equals and that they were sometimes suspected of being disloyal or untrustworthy.

'NEXT YEAR IN JERUSALEM'

For hundreds of years Jews dreamt and prayed that they would be able to celebrate 'Next Year in Jerusalem'. By the beginning of the twentieth century an increasing number of Jews were demanding a Jewish national home. By 1914, when the First World War broke out, these people were all agreed that this homeland would have to be in Palestine. This was the 'Promised Land', where the Jews (or Israelites) had lived some 2,500 years before and where several thousands still remained.

Most Jews wanted to stay in the United States, France, Britain or Germany or wherever they were living, but a small number, especially from Russia, made their way to Palestine. They bought land there and started to farm and build homes. These people and all those who believed in a Jewish national homeland were called **Zionists** because Zion is the Jewish word for Jerusalem. Between 1880 and 1914, 60,000 Zionists settled in Palestine.

During the First World War, the Zionists received great encouragement from Britain. By 1917, the British were bogged down in the fighting with Germany and they were very keen to bring the United States into the war. They believed that the Jews in America could influence their government's actions and so they declared their support for a Jewish homeland in Palestine. This declaration was made in the form of a letter to Lord Rothschild, a leading British Jew, in November 1917. It became known as the 'Balfour Declaration' because it was signed by the British Foreign Secretary, Lord Balfour.

An attack on a Jew in Russia in the late nineteenth century. The authorities appear to ignore it.

Adapted from the Balfour Declaration (from *The Jewish State*, Theodor Herzl, 1970).

Foreign Office
December 2nd, 1917

Dear Lord Rothschild,

I have much pleasure in expressing to you, on behalf of His Majesty's Government, the following declaration of sympathy with Jewish Zionist ambitions. This has been approved by the Cabinet.

'His Majesty's Government view with favour the establishment in Palestine of a national home for the Jewish people. The Government will make every effort to help bring this about. It is clearly understood that nothing shall be done which may harm the civil and religious rights of existing non-Jewish communities in Palestine, or the rights and political status enjoyed by Jews in any other country.'

I should be grateful if you would bring this declaration to the knowledge of the Zionist Federation.

[Signed by Lord Balfour]

Questions

a What was the main aim of the Zionists?
b How useful is Source A to a historian studying why some Jews wanted a homeland of their own?
c Why did the British produce the Balfour Declaration (see Source B)?

Key Issue

- What is the Arab claim to Palestine?

For many centuries the Arabs have lived in the lands which we call the Middle East. They form the majority of the population and all speak the same language, Arabic. In the seventh century AD, most of the Arabs were converted to the religion of Islam. They became followers of Muhammad and are known as Muslims. From their homeland in Arabia, they swept across the Middle East and North Africa in the seventh and eighth centuries spreading their new religion. Palestine was one of the countries they took over.

In the Middle Ages, the Arab Muslims made important discoveries in mathematics and medicine. Their merchants bought and sold goods in Europe, Africa and Asia, and their lands grew rich. Then, in the sixteenth century, the Turks (who were also Muslims but not Arabs) conquered much of the Middle East. The Arabs were forced to pay taxes and provide soldiers for their Turkish masters.

In the late nineteenth century the Arabs tried several times to remove their Turkish rulers. Their aim was to re-establish Arab rule in the Middle East, including Palestine. In 1913, the first Arab National Congress was held and, a year later, the Arab Nationalist Manifesto (see Source A) was published. This called for independence from Turkey.

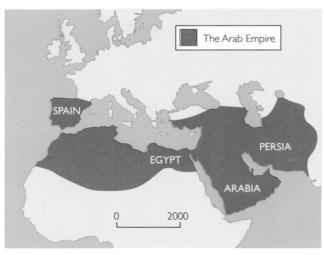

The Arab empire in the eighth century.

THE ARABS AND THE FIRST WORLD WAR

The First World War was a turning point in the Arab struggle for independence as well as in the Jewish struggle for a homeland. Turkey fought on the German side against Britain and its allies. The British were afraid that their supplies of oil from Persia (or Iran, as it's known today) might be cut off by the Turks, so they decided to encourage the Arabs to rebel against their Turkish rulers and seek independence.

The British High Commissioner in Egypt, Sir Herbert McMahon, exchanged several letters with Hussein, the Sharif of Mecca, the most important Arab Muslim leader, in 1915. Here is an extract from one of them.

Great Britain is prepared to recognise and support the independence of the Arabs. When the situation allows, Great Britain will assist the Arabs to establish what may appear to be the most suitable forms of government in those various territories.

An Arab army was raised and led by Prince Faisal, the son of the Sharif of Mecca. The army blew up Turkish trains and disrupted the flow of military supplies to the Turkish soldiers. The Arabs felt that they had fought for their independence from the Turks and now deserved complete self-government.

Arab leaders were therefore angered when they heard that Britain and France had secretly agreed in 1916 to carve up Turkey's Arab lands after the war and share them out between themselves. This agreement is known as the Sykes–Picot Agreement after the British and French politicians who made it. Some land would be directly ruled by Britain or France. The rest would be Arab states but with either Britain or France having some indirect control over them.

THE BRITISH MANDATE IN PALESTINE

In 1919, the Peace of Versailles, which followed the end of the First World War, confirmed Arab fears. As part of the peace treaty, Britain and France were given **mandates**, or orders, to govern certain countries in the Middle East until the Arab people were considered ready to govern themselves. Britain was given mandates over Palestine, Jordan and Iraq, and British troops and their administrators took control of these lands. France was granted mandates over Syria and Lebanon and soon sent troops in to take control.

SOURCE

This is an extract from the Arab National Manifesto, 1914 (from *Arab Nationalism*, S Haim, 1962).

Arise, O ye Arabs! Take out the sword from the scabbard. Do not let an oppressive tyrant, who only despises you, remain in your country; cleanse your country from those who show their hatred to you, to your race and to your language.

O ye Arabs! You all dwell in one land, you speak one language, so be also one nation and one land.

Do not become divided amongst yourselves.

B SOURCE

Arab soldiers like these blew up Turkish trains and disrupted the flow of military supplies to the Turkish army (1918).

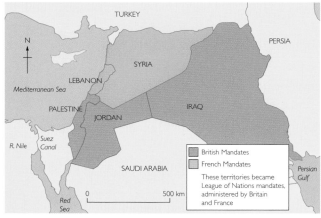

The Middle East after the First World War showing the British and French mandates.

Questions

a Give one reason why, in the First World War, the British said they would support independence for the Arabs.

b Explain what Source A tells us about the Arab desire for independence at the beginning of the twentieth century.

c Why was the First World War a turning point in the struggle for Arab independence?

d How useful is Source B to a historian studying the Arab role in the First World War?

e Britain made 'promises' to the Jews, the Arabs and the French in the war. Which of these peoples would feel most betrayed after the war? You should refer in your answer to:
  • the McMahon letter, 1915
  • the Sykes–Picot Agreement, 1916
  • the Balfour Declaration, 1917
  • the British mandate over Palestine.

Key Issue

- Why did British rule lead to an Arab rebellion?

THE BRITISH MANDATE IN PALESTINE

In 1917 British troops entered Jerusalem, the capital of Palestine, driving out the Turks. In 1919 Britain was given a **mandate** to govern Palestine. For the next 30 years the British government was to rule the country.

The Arabs of Palestine felt that they had simply exchanged Turkish rulers for British ones. Like the Arabs of Syria and Iraq, they were frustrated and disappointed that they had not been given their independence.

The Palestinian Arabs were even more angered by increasing Jewish **immigration** and the fact that Jews were buying land in 'their' country. The Jews only bought land in a few areas of Palestine, but in these areas the Arabs claimed they were being driven out. They also accused the British of being pro-**Zionist**.

ARAB-JEWISH RIOTS

In 1921 an Arab mob attacked the Jews in the town of Jaffa (see the map opposite). This was the main port of arrival for Jewish immigrants. Just to the north of the town was Tel Aviv, the largest Jewish **settlement** in Palestine. After two days of rioting, 200 Jews and 120 Arabs were dead or wounded.

The British authorities immediately stopped all Jewish immigration. The Arabs were told that only a part of Palestine was to be made into a Jewish

British troops enter Jerusalem, 1917.

Making a home in the 'Promised Land'. A Jewish couple, recent immigrants from Europe, build a home in Palestine, 1935.

national home. Soon afterwards, immigration began again but the British insisted it would be limited. The Arabs asked the British government to make Palestine independent as they hoped that the Arab majority would be able to dominate the Jewish minority. When Winston Churchill, a government minister, visited Palestine in 1921, a group of Arab leaders asked him to go against the Balfour Declaration and stop immigration. Churchill replied:

You ask me to reject the Balfour Declaration and to stop immigration. This is not in my power and it is not my wish.

The British government seemed unable to satisfy either Jews or Arabs. The rate of immigration slowed down in the 1920s, and yet the Jewish population still doubled in the ten years after the war. By 1929 there were a million Arabs and 160,000 Jews living in Palestine whereas, in 1919, there had only been 60,000 Jews (see bar graph on page 8).

In 1929 violence erupted again. This time it started in the city of Jerusalem, which is a holy city for Jews but also for Muslims. In the 1920s there was continuous tension in the city and some Arab leaders claimed that the Jews intended to take over some of the Arab (Muslim) holy places. In August large Arab

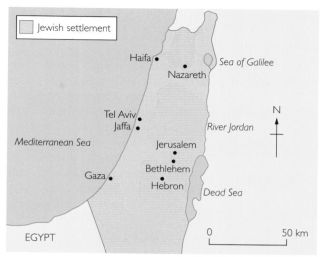
The main areas of Jewish settlement in Palestine in the 1920s.

crowds attacked Jews inside and outside the city. The attacks spread throughout Palestine and, in four days, 133 Jews were killed (60 of these deaths were in the town of Hebron). During the attacks, 116 Arabs were also killed, mostly by the British police while trying to stop the anti-Jewish violence.

The Dome of the Rock and the Wailing Wall in Jerusalem. Muslims believe that Muhammad rose to heaven from the Rock. Just below it, in the foreground, is the Western or 'Wailing' Wall, which Jews believe to be the last remaining part of the ancient Jewish Temple.

NAZI ANTI-SEMITISM AND JEWISH IMMIGRATION

Similar outbreaks of violence, although not so widespread, continued in the early 1930s, especially after 1933. In that year Adolf Hitler came to power in Germany and Nazi **anti-Semitism** drove many Jews abroad. Thousands fled to Palestine and by 1939 there were nearly 450,000 Jews in the country. Tension remained high and British government reports all came to the same conclusion – that the Arabs were afraid of losing their country as more and more of them became 'landless and discontented'.

The British therefore planned to restrict immigration and land sales. This caused uproar among the Jews in Europe and America as well as in Palestine, so the plan was put aside. The British were in an impossible position. If they allowed unrestricted immigration, Arab fears and violence would increase. But if they stopped or controlled immigration, the world would accuse them of inhumanity, of not caring for the Jews who were being **persecuted** by the Nazis.

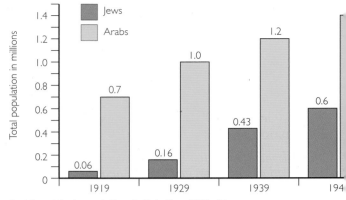

Jewish and Arab populations in Palestine, 1919–47.

ARAB REBELLION, 1936–39

In 1936, widespread fighting broke out as armed Arab bands attacked Jewish settlements. The British responded harshly. They hanged several Arab leaders and destroyed houses suspected of containing Arab terrorists or arms. They also helped to organise the Jewish Defence Force, the **Haganah** (which was set up in the 1920s and was later to develop into the Israeli army).

Orde Wingate was a British officer who trained Jewish squads to attack Arab villages during the

Arab fighters, 1938. This picture was found on the body of an Arab rebel leader who was killed by British troops.

rebellion. He was an effective military leader, but also a very cruel one.

Wingate went up to the four Arab prisoners. He said in Arabic, 'You have arms in the village. Where have you hidden them?' The Arabs shook their heads. Wingate reached down and took sand from the ground. He thrust it into the mouth of the first Arab and pushed it down until he puked. 'Now', he said, 'Where have you hidden the arms?' Still they shook their heads. Wingate turned to one of the Jews and, pointing to the coughing Arab, said, 'Shoot this man'. The Jew looked at him and hesitated. Wingate said in a tense voice, 'Did you hear? Shoot this man.' The Jew shot the Arab. The others stared in horror at the dead body. The Jewish boys looked in silence. 'Now speak,' said Wingate. They spoke.

PEEL COMMISSION, 1937

In 1937, the British government set up an inquiry, led by Lord Peel. In their report, the Peel Commission recommended the **partition** (division) of Palestine into two separate states, one Jewish and a second Arab state. The Arabs rejected it and the fighting continued. With the help of more troops, better weapons and transport, the British forces gradually regained control of Palestine.

By 1939, when the rebellion ended, the British government had given up all further ideas of partition. It declared that Britain would continue to rule Palestine. It also said that it would restrict Jewish immigration.

For each of the next five years a limit of 10,000 Jewish immigrants will be allowed ... apart from a special quota in the near future of 25,000 refugees as a contribution to the solution of the Jewish refugee problem.

After the period of five years no further Jewish immigration will be permitted unless the Arabs are prepared to agree to it.

The British government adopted this policy because war was approaching and it feared the growth of friendship between Arab leaders and Germany. Britain needed to keep the friendship of the Arab countries so that oil supplies from the Middle East would continue to reach Britain.

A SOURCE

This comes from a note written by Lord Balfour, in 1919, at the Peace Conference after the end of the First World War.

In Palestine we do not propose to go through the form of consulting the wishes of the present inhabitants of the country. Zionism, be it right or wrong, good or bad, is rooted in age-long traditions of far greater meaning than the desires and prejudices of the 700,000 Arabs who now inhabit that ancient land.

B SOURCE

In 1922, the **League of Nations** confirmed Britain's mandate in Palestine (from *The Israel–Arab Reader*, Walter Laqueur, 1969).

Britain shall be responsible for placing the country under such political, administrative and economic conditions as will secure the establishment of the Jewish national home and the development of self-governing institutions, and also for safeguarding the civil and religious rights of all the inhabitants of Palestine no matter what their race or religion.

C SOURCE

A British government official describes how he had to order poor Arab peasants to leave land that had recently been bought by the Jews (from *The Middle East*, Walter Oppenheim, 1989).

It was a large stretch of land inhabited by Arabs in tents. Eventually, after a long court case, it was decided that they must be evicted. I had the dreadful job of going in with the police, knocking down their tents, and turning them off.

Questions

a **Why were Palestinian Arabs angry about Jews emigrating to Palestine after the First World War?**

b **Sources A and B give different views of the Arab inhabitants of Palestine. Why do you think they are different?**

c **How useful is Source C in explaining why the Arab rebellion broke out in 1936?**

d **Why was Britain unable to establish an independent Palestine state ruled jointly by Jews and Arabs? You may use the following information to help you with your answer:**
 • **Jewish immigration**
 • **Arab rebellion**
 • **the importance of oil.**

Why did the Arabs rebel in 1936? Write a few sentences under each of these headings:
● The British mandate in Palestine
● Jewish immigration
● British rule in Palestine.

Key Issue

- Why did the British leave Palestine in 1948?

JEWISH TERRORISM

The King David Hotel in Jerusalem housed the British military headquarters in Palestine. It was protected by barbed wire, machine guns and patrolling soldiers. At noon on 22 July 1946, a lorry drove up to the entrance of the hotel kitchen. Men dressed as Arabs got out and unloaded their cargo of milk churns. They rolled them into the building. No one guessed that the milk churns contained high explosives or that the 'Arabs' were members of **Irgun**, a Jewish terrorist group. At 12.37p.m. the explosion tore through the building killing 88 people, including 15 Jews.

Outrages like this were the result of hatred of British rule which developed amongst the Jews in Palestine. When they heard of the deaths of millions of Jews in the Nazi **Holocaust**, **Zionists** began to demand that the Jews in Palestine should be granted their own independent state. They wanted a flag and an army of their own. They wanted a state where the survivors of Nazi persecution could live in peace.

During the Second World War, many Palestinian Jews fought in the British army, but after the war they became impatient with British rule. Jewish

The King David Hotel was blown up by members of Irgun, a Jewish terrorist group, in July 1946.

This photograph appeared on the front page of the Daily Express *in August 1947. It shows two British soldiers who had been hanged by members of Irgun. This hanging was in revenge for the execution of three of Irgun's members.*

leaders in Palestine thought the British were stopping them from having their own independent state. For this reason, Jewish terrorists began to bomb British army bases, barracks, bridges, trains and railways in Palestine. Between 1945 and 1948 over 300 British soldiers or officials were killed in Palestine.

INTERNATIONAL PRESSURE ON BRITAIN

Despite such acts by Jewish terrorists, there was widespread sympathy in Europe and the United States for the Jews who had survived the Nazi concentration camps. The large Jewish population in the United States gave millions of dollars to Zionist leaders and forced US President Truman to put pressure on the British. Truman said Britain should allow 100,000 Jewish **refugees** to enter Palestine. The British government refused, claiming that it

would be unfair to the Arabs. British leaders said it would lead to **civil war** in Palestine.

The British continued to stop boatloads of illegal Jewish immigrants from landing in Palestine. In 1947, for example, a ship called *The Exodus*, carrying 4,500 refugees from Europe, was prevented from landing its passengers and was sent back to Europe. As a result of actions like these, the British authorities came in for worldwide criticism.

BRITAIN HANDS OVER TO THE UNITED NATIONS

The British were also exhausted after the war, with food shortages and rationing at home, and could hardly afford to keep 100,000 troops in Palestine. After 30 years of trying to solve the problems of Palestine, the British government announced, at the end of 1947, that it would hand over Palestine to the **United Nations** (UN).

The *Theodor Herzl* refugee ship arrived in Palestine with 25,000 illegal refugees on board. The banner on the ship reads, 'The Germans destroyed our families and homes – don't you destroy our hopes.'

This cartoon appeared in the *Daily Mail* in September 1947. The figure on the left represents an Arab and the figure on the right a Jew.

Questions

a Why did the events of the Holocaust make it difficult for Britain to control Jewish **immigration** into Palestine after 1945?

b How useful is Source A as evidence of Zionist attitudes towards British rule in Palestine after 1945?

c Explain what Source B tells us about why the British decided to hand over Palestine to the UN.

d 'The photograph in Source A is more reliable as evidence for the historian studying the end of British rule in Palestine than the cartoon in Source B.' Do you agree? Explain your answer.

5 PARTITION AND THE BIRTH OF ISRAEL

Key Issue

• Why was the birth of Israel so bloody?

UN PARTITION PLAN

In November 1947 the **United Nations** voted to divide Palestine and set up both a Jewish and an Arab state. The areas that were mainly Jewish (in population and land ownership) were allocated to the Jewish state and those that were mainly Arab were allocated to the Arab state. As you can see on the map below, this resulted in a criss-cross arrangement with 'kissing points' at the intersections. The UN thought that this would force the two sides to co-operate!

The Palestinian Arabs rejected this plan, especially as the Jews were to be given the larger area. The Arabs did not wish to give up their land.

They felt that the western powers should find a home for the Jews elsewhere. After all, the Arabs were not responsible for the **Holocaust**.

Palestinian Jews accepted the plan but not all of them were happy with it. This was because many Jewish **settlements** were to be included in the Arab state and the holy city of Jerusalem was to be controlled by an international force. Menachem Begin, leader of **Irgun**, announced:

*The **partition** of the homeland is illegal. It will never be recognised. It will not bind the Jewish people. Jerusalem was and will for ever be our capital.*

WHAT CAUSED THE ARAB FLIGHT?

After the publication of the partition plan, fighting between Arabs and Jews grew worse. There was a particularly bitter struggle to control the roads leading to Jerusalem and massacres of civilians were carried out by both sides. Soldiers from Syria and Iraq began to cross into Palestine to help the Arabs, while the **Haganah** organised Jewish defence forces.

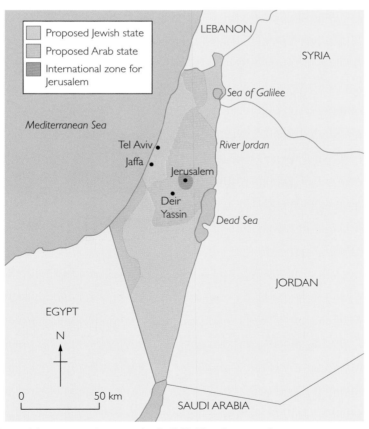

The UN Partition Plan. What problems might you expect in a state that is divided into three parts?

WANTED! This is a photograph of Menachem Begin which was published by the British authorities in Palestine. A reward was offered for information leading to his arrest. Begin, who had lost both his parents and a brother in Nazi concentration camps, was the leader of Irgun. Irgun was responsible for bombing the King David Hotel (see page 10).

By 14 May 1948, when the British finally withdrew, over 300,000 Arabs had fled from what was to become the new Jewish state. Arabs and Jews have argued about the causes of this flight ever since.

In the weeks before the British withdrawal from Palestine, some of the bloodiest fighting took place in and around Jerusalem. In one incident, on 10 April 1948, Irgun fighters attacked the village of Deir Yassin (which was inside what was to be Arab territory under the UN partition plan) and killed the inhabitants. They said they believed it was an Arab headquarters. The following sources focus on Deir Yassin and the reasons for the Arab flight.

Arab refugees flee from their homes in 1947.

SOURCE

Menachem Begin, the Irgun leader, wrote a book called *The Revolt* in 1951. This is an extract from it.

The civilian population of Deir Yassin was actually given a warning by us before the battle began. The fire of the enemy was murderous. Our men were compelled to fight for every house: to overcome the enemy they used large numbers of hand-grenades.

*Throughout the Arab world and the world at large, a wave of lying **propaganda** was let loose about 'Jewish atrocities' . . . the Arabs began to flee in terror, even before they clashed with Jewish forces . . . This Arab propaganda spread a legend of terror amongst Arabs and Arab troops, who were seized with panic at the mention of Irgun soldiers. The legend was worth half a dozen battalions to the forces of Israel.*

D **SOURCE**

Erskine Childers, an Irish journalist, wrote in the *Spectator* in 1961.

I next decided to test the charge that the Arab evacuation orders were broadcast by Arab radio – which could be done thoroughly because the BBC monitored all Middle East broadcasts throughout 1948. The records, and companion ones by a US monitoring unit, can be seen at the British Museum.

There was not a single order, or appeal, or suggestion about evacuation from Palestine from any Arab radio station, inside or outside Palestine in 1948. There is a repeated monitored record of Arab appeal, even flat orders, to the civilians of Palestine to stay put.

B **SOURCE**

This is the view of the Britain/Israel Public Affairs Centre, an Israeli information service. It was published in the 1980s.

If the Arabs were so attached to their land, why did they leave it during a crisis? The blame must belong to Arab leaders who, expecting a quick victory by their combined armies over Israel, encouraged Arabs to leave Palestine, promising that on their return they would be able to claim the property of the Jews as well. Arab propaganda led them to fear what would happen to them if they stayed, and threatened that they would also be considered traitors to the Arab cause.

Q **uestions**

a Give one reason to explain why the bloodiest fighting took place around Jerusalem.
b How useful is Source A to the historian studying the reasons for Arab flight?
c Sources B and D give different views of the Arab flight from Palestine. Why do you think they are different?
d Why did so many Arabs flee from Palestine before the British left in May 1948?

C **SOURCE**

S. Penrose, a British historian, wrote:

*There is no doubt that frightful massacres such as that which took place at Deir Yassin in April 1948 were carried out for the major purpose of frightening the Arab population and causing them to take flight. The **Zionist** radio repeated incessantly for the benefit of Arab listeners 'Remember Deir Yassin!'*

6 THE WAR OF 1948–49

Key Issue

- How did Israel survive its first war?

When the state of Israel was created, none of the Arab states recognised its right to exist. As far as they were concerned, Palestine had been occupied by **Zionists** and Israel ought to be destroyed. Over the next 25 years there were to be four major wars between Israel and its Arab neighbours. This and the next five chapters examine the causes and consequences of each of those wars. They also explain why much bigger Arab states have been unable to defeat the Israelis on the battlefield.

THE INVASION OF ISRAEL, MAY 1948

On 14 May 1948, the new state of Israel was proclaimed. Immediately, armies from the Arab states of Egypt, Syria, Jordan, Lebanon and Iraq invaded.

The Arabs of Palestine were disorganised and lacked good leaders. Many of the armies from the other Arab states were poorly trained or badly equipped. They certainly had no co-ordinated plan of campaign. The only efficient and experienced Arab force was the Arab Legion from Jordan. It captured and held the eastern part, the Old City, of Jerusalem.

On the other fronts, the Israelis resisted and the **United Nations** ordered a ceasefire in June. The Israelis now reorganised and acquired fresh weapons. Fighting broke out twice more and, by January 1949, Israel had driven out the Arab armies and even occupied some of the land that the UN had granted to the Arabs (see map opposite). In addition, about 700,000 Palestinian Arabs had fled their homes. Israel refused to hand back the land it had occupied in the fighting, while the Arab governments refused to accept that the state of Israel existed. There was no peace treaty, only a truce.

HOW DID ISRAEL SURVIVE?

The Israeli state had survived its first great test because the Jews had defended it fiercely and suc-

cessfully in the war. Jewish soldiers were disciplined and hardened by their experience in fighting with the British in the Second World War and against them after it. They were well-led and organised. Above all, they were fighting to save their new country.

The people of Israel realised that they were surrounded by enemies. They were convinced that the Arabs wished to drive them into the sea and would try to attack again. Soon after the fighting ended in 1949, the Secretary of the Arab League, which represents all Arab states, said:

As long as we don't make peace with the Zionists the war is not over. And as long as the war is not over there is neither winner nor loser. As soon as we recognise the existence of Israel, we admit, by this act, that we are defeated.

The Israeli army would have to be constantly on the alert and most Israeli men were liable to be called up for **military service**. The Israeli army helped to shape the new nation as well as defend it. The Jews of Israel had come from different parts of Europe and the USA. Between 1949 and 1954 another 700,000 arrived. Many were from North Africa and other parts of the Middle East. In the army they all received a similar training, lived

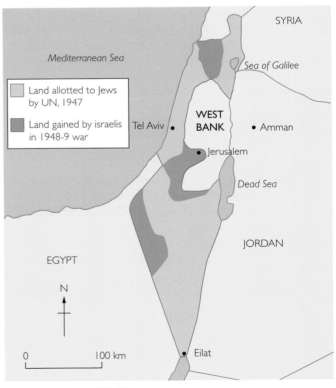

Israeli gains in the 1948–49 war.

together and had to learn Hebrew, the Jewish language. It was experience in the army that helped to make the newly arrived Jews into true Israelis.

Many Israelis went to live and work on **kibbutzim.** These were (and still are) large co-operative farms in which all the property and work was shared. Different families ate together and shared living quarters.

With financial aid from the United States and Germany, the Israelis irrigated and cultivated vast areas of desert. They established chemical, shipbuilding and motor industries.

A NATION ON GUARD

Israel is a small country and none of the Israelis felt really safe from attack. They feared that the Palestinian Arabs, most of whom had left Israel, would try to win back the lands they had lost. Nearly half a million Arabs had fled to the two areas of Palestine that were not taken over by Israel. These two areas were the West Bank, which was protected by the state of Jordan, and Gaza, a thin strip of land controlled by the Egyptians. Palestinian fighters, or **fedayeen**, on the West Bank and in Gaza carried out raids into Israeli territory. The Israelis **retaliated** fiercely.

A SOURCE

Palestinian Arab troops, 1948.

Questions

a How useful are the photographs in Sources A and B for an understanding of the outcome of the 1948–49 war?

b How was Israel able to defeat her Arab opponents in the 1948–49 war? You should refer in your answer to:
  • Israeli strengths
  • Arab weaknesses.

c In what ways did the Israeli army help to shape the new nation?

B SOURCE

Israeli Jewish troops, 1948.

Key Issue

- What caused the outbreak of a second Arab–Israeli War?

THE ARAB REACTION TO DEFEAT AGAINST ISRAEL

The Arab states were shocked by their defeat at the hands of the Israelis in 1948–49. It showed how weak and divided they were. It made them bitterly anti-western. The Arabs felt that the United States had bullied the **United Nations** into creating the new state of Israel. They suspected that the western powers, such as Britain, France and the USA, would use Israel as a base from which to keep an eye on the Arab states.

Also, the Arab governments were still not completely independent, even after the Second World War. The **mandates** had ended but there were still many western troops and advisers in the Middle East. For instance, in Egypt, which was the most powerful Arab state, there were 70,000 British troops in the Suez Canal area. The Canal was owned and run by the British and French. It was a vital route for oil supplies to the West.

A group of young Egyptian army officers was determined to get rid of the British troops and achieve full independence for their country. In 1952, after years of planning, they overthrew the

Colonel Nasser was one of the army officers who overthrew the unpopular Egyptian King and his government in 1952. In 1954 he became President of Egypt.

unpopular monarchy and took control of the government. Their leader was General Neguib, but the real organiser was Colonel Nasser.

NASSER

In 1954 Nasser became President and, after long discussions, he persuaded the British to withdraw their troops from the Suez Canal zone. Britain and the United States still wished to keep on good terms with Nasser. They wanted Arab support in the Middle East against the **USSR** (communist Russia). They particularly wanted an alliance with Egypt as it was the strongest, most developed Arab nation, and because the Suez Canal passed through its territory.

Nasser wanted Egypt to be neutral and was not willing to join an anti-Russian alliance. He did, however, need arms to strengthen Egypt's army. This became very urgent in February 1955 when the Israeli government decided to hit back at Egypt for encouraging Palestinian raids into Israel. Israeli troops attacked the Egyptian army headquarters in Gaza and killed 50 Egyptian soldiers. For three days Palestinian **refugees** in Gaza ran riot and demanded: 'Arms, give us arms, we shall defend ourselves!' In Cairo, the Egyptian capital, the crowds wanted revenge too.

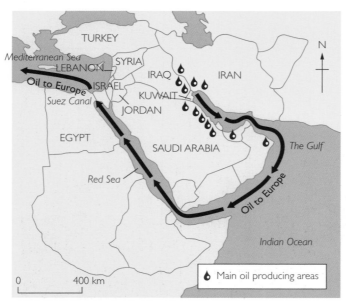

The Suez Canal oil route from the Middle East to Europe.

THE SUEZ CRISIS, 1956

In September 1955, Nasser shocked the West by agreeing to buy Russian arms from Czechoslovakia (a communist ally of the Russians). Britain and the United States thought they could still control Nasser because he depended on them for money to build the Aswan High Dam. This was a huge project on the River Nile which would create hydro-electric power for Egyptian industry and allow vast areas of land to be irrigated. In July 1956, Britain and the USA refused to lend Egypt any more money. Perhaps they hoped to persuade Nasser to co-operate. Maybe they thought they could force the Egyptians to replace him.

The Aswan High Dam being built across the River Nile, 1964.

NATIONALISATION OF THE SUEZ CANAL, JULY 1956

Again, however, Nasser shocked the West. He was not going to be pushed around any longer. He would prove that Egypt was independent now. Before a huge crowd, on 26 July, he announced that the Suez Canal was 'our Canal'. He told the crowd: 'We dug the Canal with our lives, our skulls, our bones, our blood.' Egypt would **nationalise** it and Egyptians would run it themselves. They would use the profits to build the Aswan Dam. He said that Britain and France could 'choke on their rage'. This daring act thrilled the Arabs in Egypt and elsewhere.

Britain and France were furious. The British Prime Minister, Anthony Eden, was determined not to let Nasser 'have his thumb on our windpipe'. The British and French withdrew their pilots who guided ships through the Canal. But the Egyptians kept it running and the traffic increased.

BRITISH, FRENCH AND ISRAELIS MEET IN SECRET, OCTOBER 1956

On 24 October the British and French Foreign Ministers secretly met the Israeli Prime Minister, David Ben-Gurion, in France. Ben-Gurion wished to teach the Egyptians a lesson. He wanted to end the border raids from Gaza and force Egypt to recognise the state of Israel. He also wanted to break the Egyptian **blockade** of the Tiran Straits, which prevented Israeli ships from reaching the port of Eilat (see map on page 22). Furthermore, he was worried about the increasing military strength of Egypt and the fact that the armies of Egypt, Syria and Jordan had been put under the same command.

France, like Britain and Israel, also wanted to teach Egypt, especially Nasser, a lesson. Nasser had been sending aid to the Algerians in their fight against French rule. There were other high-level meetings between Britain, France and Israel. Although it was denied at the time, a joint campaign against Egypt was being planned.

A SOURCE

Nasser explained why Egypt agreed to buy Russian arms from Czechoslovakia in September 1955 (from *The Middle East, 1914–1979*, T.G. Fraser, 1980).

I told the British and US Ambassadors last June that, if their countries did not supply me with arms, I would have to obtain them from the USSR. I stated that it was not possible for me to remain silent while Israel imported weapons for her army from several sources and posed a constant threat to us.

B SOURCE

In his speech in July 1956, Nasser justified the nationalisation of the Suez Canal (from *The Middle East, 1914–1979*, T.G. Fraser, 1980).

The canal is a part of Egypt and we are the ones who should ensure freedom of shipping. We shall continue to protect the canal.

People of Egypt. We shall maintain our independence and sovereignty. The Suez Canal Company has become our property and the Egyptian flag flies over it. We shall defend it with our blood and strength, and we shall meet aggression with aggression and evil with evil.

C SOURCE

In September 1956, the British Prime Minister, Anthony Eden, wrote to the US President (from *Full Circle*, Anthony Eden, 1960).

The seizure of the Suez Canal is, we are convinced, the opening move in a planned campaign designed by Nasser to expel all western influence and interests from Arab countries. He believes that if he can get away with this, his prestige in Arabia will be so great that [Arab] governments will have to place their united oil resources under the control of a united Arabia led by Egypt and under Russian influence. When that moment comes Nasser can deny oil to western Europe and we here shall all be at his mercy.

D SOURCE

This cartoon was published in Britain after Nasser nationalised the Suez Canal.

E SOURCE

An extract from the diary of Moshe Dayan, an Israeli Army General, 25 October 1956.

Planned meetings, some with people overseas, started about two months ago. This is now the position:

1. The Prime Minister, David Ben-Gurion, has approved the campaign and its aims.

2. Our forces will attack at dusk on 29 October 1956 and we must capture the Sinai peninsula in seven to ten days.

3. The plan is based on the assumption that British and French forces are about to act against Egypt.

4. According to information in our possession the Anglo-French forces aim to attack on 31 October 1956. Their aim is to get control of the Suez Canal Zone.

F SOURCE

This is from the Russian newspaper *Pravda*, 2 November 1956.

Defying the United Nations' Charter and international law, the Anglo-French imperialists have attacked the independent Egyptian Republic. They are trying to seize the Suez Canal and to occupy Egypt. The Israeli attack on Egypt was just the first step in the plot by England, France and Israel to spread their control to all Arab states.

Questions

a Explain what Source A tells us about Nasser's reasons for buying Russian arms.

b Sources B and C give different views on the nationalisation of the Suez Canal. Why do you think they are different?

c How useful is Source D for a historian studying the causes of the Suez crisis of 1956?

d Why did Israel want to go to war with Egypt?

e Which of Sources E and F gives the more reliable evidence of a plot between Israel, Britain and France to attack Egypt in 1956? Explain your answer using both the sources and your own knowledge.

f 'Nasser's actions were the main cause of the Suez War of 1956.' Use the sources and your own knowledge to explain whether you agree with this view.

g Why did Britain and France become involved in the 1956 Suez War? You may use the following information to help you with your answer:
   • September 1955: Nasser's purchase of Russian arms
   • July 1956: Nationalisation of the Suez Canal
   • October 1956: Secret meetings with the Israelis.

Key Issue

- Who won and who lost the war?

On 29 October 1956, Israeli forces invaded Egypt. They advanced across Sinai towards the Suez Canal (see map below). The next day, the governments of Britain and France ordered Egypt and Israel to cease fighting and withdraw ten miles from the Canal. If either side refused, the British and French would use force. The Israelis were still a long way from the Canal and they agreed, but the Egyptians refused to withdraw from the Canal because it was Egyptian territory.

On 31 October, British and French planes bombed Egyptian airfields and destroyed most of their air force. They also bombed Port Said, the city at the northern end of the Canal (see the photograph opposite). On 5 November, British and French troops landed at Port Said and advanced along the Canal. Egypt responded by sinking ships that were filled with concrete in order to obstruct the British and French advance along the Canal.

THE UNITED NATIONS STEPS IN

At the **United Nations**, the Arab states condemned the Anglo-French action. They halted oil supplies to the West. Even worse for Britain was the fact that its strongest ally, the United States, condemned the action. The US government was furious that Britain and France had used force. The Americans believed the Anglo-French action would lose the support of Arab states at a time when America was keen to win and make friends in the Arab world. The US government threatened to cut off financial aid to Britain, which would ruin the economy. The Russians went further and threatened to use military force. On 6 November, the UN declared a ceasefire and sent an emergency force to the Canal. The British and French were forced to withdraw.

NASSER, LEADER OF THE ARAB WORLD

Nasser, the Egyptian leader, became the hero of the Arab world. He had stood up to Britain and France, who had dominated the Middle East for so long, and he had gained complete control of the Suez Canal. He lost territory when the Israelis captured Sinai, but they were persuaded, by the Americans, to withdraw in 1957. In addition, Nasser could claim that the Egyptian army had only been defeated because the Israelis had British and French support.

One of the main effects of the Suez crisis was to make many of the Arab states more anti-western and more willing to seek Russian aid. The **USSR** now began to supply most of Egypt's weapons and to pay for the building of the Aswan Dam and many other projects. However, Nasser did not want Egypt to be tied to Russia and he was certainly not a communist. He wanted Egypt and the other Arab states to be neutral.

In 1964, Nasser invited the leaders of the Arab states to a conference in Cairo. Although many of them mistrusted each other, one thing united them all: opposition to the state of Israel and support for the Palestinians.

ISRAELI GAINS

The Israelis also made gains. When they withdrew from Sinai, UN troops moved in to guard the border between Egypt and Israel. In particular, UN forces were sent to Gaza to prevent more raids on Israel and to Sharm el-Sheikh to guard the passage of Israeli shipping through the Straits of Tiran.

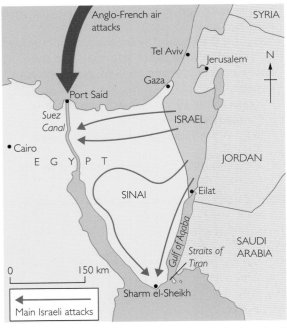

The 1956 Suez War. The Straits of Tiran were Israel's outlet to trade with Asia and Africa.

Port Said, at the northern end of the Suez Canal, was bombed by the British navy before troops landed.

A SOURCE

This is the view of an American historian, William Polk, (from *The Elusive Peace*, 1979).

Curiously, in western eyes, the Suez War made Nasser a hero. One of its purposes was to destroy him and at the beginning of the fighting few would have given him even odds to survive. However, he did; more than that, he claimed a political victory within a military defeat.

B SOURCE

Moshe Dayan, an Israeli army general, wrote this in his memoirs, *The Story of My Life*, 1976.

*It may be said right away that the three main purposes were achieved: our ships could now use the Gulf of Aqaba (leading to Eilat); an end to **fedayeen** terrorism; and the prevention of a joint attack on Israel by the Egypt-Syria-Jordan military command. In addition, the victory in Sinai meant that Israel emerged as a state that would be welcomed as a friend and ally. Further, Nasser learned to respect the power of Israel's army.*

C SOURCE

Nasser, writing later, sums up the results of the war.

After Suez, we were able to take over all the foreign property in our country and therefore the Suez War regained the wealth of the Egyptian people to be used in the interests of the Egyptian people. Then, of course, it was clear for the Egyptian people that they could defend their country and secure its independence.

Questions

a How useful is Source A to a historian studying the Suez War? Use Source A and your own knowledge to answer the question.

b Sources B and C give different views of the results of the Suez War of 1956. Why do you think they are different?

c 'The Israelis gained little from the war because they had to withdraw from the land they had conquered.' Use the sources, and your own knowledge, to explain whether you agree with this view.

Make brief notes on each of the following:
- The key features of the Suez War
- The UN's role in ending the War and restoring peace
- How Nasser became the hero of the Arab world after the War
- Why Britain and France were forced to withdraw from Suez.

> **Key Issue**
> - Who was to blame for the war?

A young Fatah member being trained in the use of his weapon. Raids by Fatah and Israeli reprisals contributed to the tension, leading to war in 1967.

PALESTINE LIBERATION ORGANISATION

At their meeting in Cairo in 1964, leaders of the Arab states decided to set up the Palestine Liberation Organisation (**PLO**). The aim of this organisation was to win back the land that the Palestinians had lost in 1948–49. In 1965, a **guerrilla** group called **Fatah**, which was part of the PLO, carried out its first raid on Israel. This group carried out many armed raids on Israel over the next few years. It also planted bombs in Israeli government buildings and planted mines on roads.

AMERICAN AID TO ISRAEL

The state of Israel had become richer and more modern since the 1956 war. Industries had been built and huge areas of desert irrigated. Israel had also spent vast sums of money on its armed forces to defend itself. This was possible only with huge gifts from abroad. Most of this aid came from the United States. In fact, the US government and American Jews sent about $1000 million a year to Israel. The US government felt that Israel was a close, firm friend in a troubled part of the world and it knew that Russia was arming Egypt and Syria.

TENSION RISES, 1966–67

Fatah had its bases in three countries: Syria, Jordan and Lebanon. All three bordered Israel. Israeli villages were often attacked by Fatah guerrillas. The governments of Lebanon and Jordan tried to restrict PLO activities because they were afraid of Israeli **reprisals**. The Syrians, however, were very keen to support the PLO. They encouraged Fatah's raids against Israel, and supplied men and arms. The only neighbouring state from which Israel was not attacked was Egypt. This was because **United Nations** troops had been placed on the border

between Egypt and Israel after the 1956 war to prevent further clashes.

In 1966 the Syrians became even more anti-Israel and accused the Egyptian government of not supporting them. They taunted Nasser, saying that he was hiding behind the protection of the UN troops. Nasser was deeply hurt. He wanted his country to remain peaceful, but he also wanted to remain the leader of the Arab world. So, in November 1966, he signed a defence agreement with the Syrian government whereby if one state was attacked, the other would come to its defence.

Tension was not only high in Syria, for a week later a mine exploded on the Israel–Jordan frontier, killing three Israeli soldiers. The Israelis **retaliated** by attacking the nearest Jordanian village. In early 1967 there were many more raids and reprisals across the borders. Israeli villages near the Syrian border were frequently shelled by Syrian guns. In April 1967 the Israeli air force shot down six Syrian fighter planes after a Syrian attack on northern Israel.

THE CRISIS OF MAY 1967

On 11 May, Russia warned its Syrian ally that Israel was building up its armed forces on the Syrian border, ready to attack. This was not true. The

Russian government was either mistaken or it was lying. Nevertheless, the story spread rapidly and Nasser moved 100,000 Egyptian troops to Sinai (see map below). On 18 May, Nasser asked the UN commander to remove his troops from Egyptian soil. He wanted to prove that Egypt was completely independent. The UN forces could stay on Egyptian territory only as long as Egypt allowed them. The UN Secretary-General proposed that the UN troops be placed on the Israeli side of the border. The Israelis refused, so the UN troops were withdrawn.

The PLO and the leaders of Syria, Jordan and Iraq now challenged Nasser to take control of the Gulf of Aqaba again. On 22 May, Egypt closed the Gulf of Aqaba to Israeli shipping. The Israelis regarded this as 'an act of aggression' against Israel, and claimed that the United States, France and Britain had 'guaranteed' free passage for all shipping through the Gulf of Aqaba in 1957.

Meanwhile, a war fever was being whipped up in the press and on the radio in several Arab states. In Iraq, the President spoke on the radio:

The existence of Israel is an error which we must put right. This is our opportunity to wipe out the disgrace which is Israel which has been with us since 1948. Our goal is clear – to wipe Israel off the map.

In Egypt, on 29 May, Nasser stepped up the pressure in a speech to the Egyptian parliament. He demanded that Israel should allow the Palestinian **refugees** to return to Israel and that Israel should give up the land taken in the 1948–49 war. Maybe he thought that Israel would give way and he could win a victory without a war.

In Jordan, King Hussein wanted to avoid war and remain neutral if fighting broke out. But half the population of Jordan was Palestinian, and newspapers and demonstrations demanded revenge for what had happened in 1948–49. On 30 May, King Hussein signed a defence treaty with Egypt.

War broke out a week later.

Questions

a **Give one reason to explain why the USA supported Israel.**
b **In what ways did the PLO contribute to Arab–Israeli tension in 1966–67?**
c **Describe the key events leading to the outbreak of war in June 1967.**

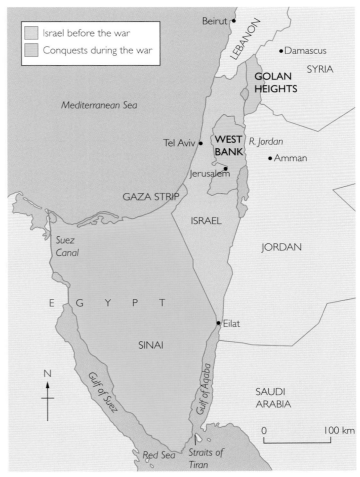

Land gained by Israel during the Six-Day War, 1967.

Israeli soldiers scramble to man their tanks, 1967.

THE OUTBREAK OF WAR, JUNE 1967

The Israelis feared a repeat of 1948. They were surrounded by warlike Arab states. They decided to attack first. Just after dawn on Monday 5 June, the Israeli air force took off. It attacked the Arab planes on the ground. Within four hours the Israelis had destroyed the air forces of Egypt, Syria and Jordan.

The war was to last six days but the Israelis had virtually won on the first day. They had complete control of the skies. The main facts of the fighting are presented in the table below.

Date	Israel v. Egypt	Israel v. Jordan	Israel v. Syria
Monday 5 June	Israeli planes bombed all 19 Egyptian airfields and wrecked 300 planes. Israeli troops advanced into the Gaza Strip and Sinai desert.	The Israelis destroyed the Jordanian air force. Jordanian troops attacked West Jerusalem.	Israeli planes crippled the Syrian air force.
Tuesday 6 June	The Israelis raced the Egyptian forces to the Suez Canal. The Israeli air force destroyed many Egyptian tanks and other vehicles, while Israeli ground forces destroyed or captured the rest.	Heavy fighting for control of Jerusalem and the West Bank of the River Jordan.	
Wednesday 7 June	The Israelis won complete control of Sinai and accepted the UN call for a ceasefire with Egypt.	The Israelis captured all of Jerusalem. Jordan accepted the UN demand for a ceasefire.	
Thursday 8 June	Egypt accepted the call for a ceasefire.	Israel won control of all the West Bank of the River Jordan.	
Friday 9 June			Israeli troops attacked the Golan Heights.
Saturday 10 June			Israelis took control of the Golan Heights. Syria accepted the UN call for a ceasefire.

A SOURCE

From a British history book written in 1976.

Who was to blame for the War? It comes down to whether you think Israel was justified in attacking Egypt when and how she did. Israel claims that the Arab powers were threatening her with destruction and were ready to attack her. Egypt had already closed the Gulf of Aqaba which she knew Israel would regard as an act of war. Israel could not afford to let the Arabs strike first for she was too small and too vulnerable.

The Arabs say that Israel should not have been in existence at all. They also say that Israel had to go to war to save its economy and ward off political instability. There is some support for this view. The Six Day war united the country and brought millions of US dollars into Israel as well as curing her unemployment problem.

B SOURCE

A cartoon published in a Lebanese Arab newspaper in May 1967. Each cannon has the name of a different Arab state on it (but the name of Egypt is not one of them).

C SOURCE

A statement made by the Deputy Commander-in-Chief of the Egyptian armed forces on 14 May 1967.

It has appeared clearly since the beginning of May 1967 that Israel is trying to direct military blows at the Arab people of Syria. In the past few days, reliable reports have shown that there are huge Israeli troop concentrations on the Syrian borders. Their intention is to overthrow the Syrian government and suppress the movement for the liberation of Palestine.

We decided to take a firm stand against the Israeli military threats and intervene immediately in case of any aggressive action taken by Israel against Syria.

D SOURCE

On 24 May 1967, the Syrian Defence Minister challenged the Israelis:

We shall never call for, nor accept peace. We have resolved to drench this land with your blood and throw you into the sea for good.

E SOURCE

On 29 May 1967, Nasser spoke to the Egyptian parliament (from The *Middle East, 1914–1979*, T.G. Fraser, 1980):

Preparations have already been made. We are now ready to confront Israel. The issue now at hand is not the Gulf of Aqaba, the Straits of Tiran, or the withdrawal of the UN forces, but the rights of the Palestine people. It is the aggression which took place in Palestine in 1948 with the collaboration of Britain and the United States.

F SOURCE

From a booklet published by the Israeli government, 1969.

In 1966–67 terrorism had been increased by the Arab states to a fearsome peak. Syrian radio continuously broadcast claims of the havoc and destruction caused by Arab terrorists in Israel. The Syrian Prime Minister said at the United Nations in October 1966: 'Syria will never retreat from the popular liberation war to recover Palestine.'

Questions

a How far do Sources A and B agree about the causes of the Six-Day War?

b How useful are Sources D and E as evidence for the causes of the Six-Day War?

c Sources C and F give different views on the origins of the Six-Day War. Why do you think they are different? Explain your answer using the sources and your own knowledge.

d 'Israel went to war to overthrow the Syrian government and suppress the movement for the liberation of Palestine.' Is this a fair interpretation of the causes of the Six-Day War? Use the sources and your own knowledge to answer this question.

Key Issue

- What did Israel gain from the War?

ISRAELIS TRIUMPHANT

The Israelis achieved a brilliant military victory in June 1967. The Arabs had lost 15,000 men while the Israelis had lost less than a thousand. The Arabs had larger armies but their air forces were destroyed. The Arabs had modern Soviet missiles and other weapons but the Israelis had the most advanced US electronic equipment and were highly skilled and well trained. Above all, the Israelis believed they were fighting for their nation's survival.

THE ARABS IN DEFEAT

The Arabs felt more hostile than ever. They blamed their defeat on the United States, Britain and other European powers, whom they accused of helping Israel in the war. The three main oil-producing Arab states of Saudi Arabia, Kuwait and Libya agreed to pay £135 million annually to Egypt and Jordan, the two states which had suffered most in the war. The Soviet Union decided to replace the weapons that its allies, Egypt and Syria, had lost. The Arabs still refused to recognise the state of Israel.

THE OCCUPIED TERRITORIES

Following their success in June 1967, the Israelis now had to win the peace. Above all, they had to decide what to do with the lands they had conquered. Chapter 13 will examine the effects of the war from a Palestinian point of view. This chapter will examine the Israeli viewpoint.

The Israelis argued with each other about the **occupied territories** – the West Bank, Gaza, Sinai and the Golan Heights. They still argue today (as you will see in Chapter 20) but most of them agreed that Jews must dominate the territories. In fact, the Israeli government decided on military occupation of the conquered lands. It also ordered the army to confiscate Arab land and to build Jewish **settlements** in order to make the areas more secure.

On one point, in particular, the Israelis were united. They had taken control of East Jerusalem, the Old City, for the first time in nearly 2,000 years. They were determined to hold on to it.

Israel's borders were now secure. There was a buffer zone, or cushion, between its land and each of its three main enemies:

- **Syria**. Villages in the north of Israel were safe from Syrian artillery now that the Israelis controlled the Golan Heights.
- **Jordan**. Military fortifications were built on the banks of the River Jordan while the land on the West Bank of the river was controlled by Israel.
- **Egypt.** The Sinai desert formed a huge buffer between Israel and the Egyptian army.

Victorious Israeli soldiers at the Western Wall in Jerusalem, 1967. The Wall is the one remaining part of the ancient Jewish temple that was destroyed by the Romans.

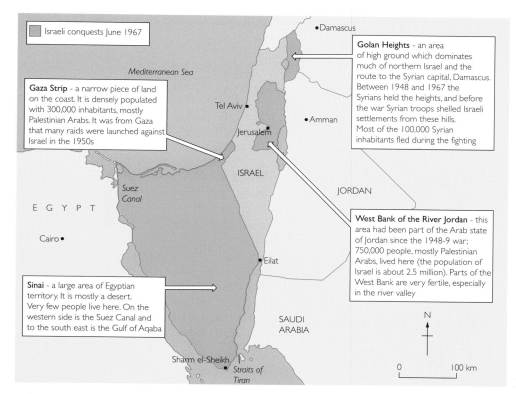

Gaza Strip - a narrow piece of land on the coast. It is densely populated with 300,000 inhabitants, mostly Palestinian Arabs. It was from Gaza that many raids were launched against Israel in the 1950s

Golan Heights - an area of high ground which dominates much of northern Israel and the route to the Syrian capital, Damascus. Between 1948 and 1967 the Syrians held the heights, and before the war Syrian troops shelled Israeli settlements from these hills. Most of the 100,000 Syrian inhabitants fled during the fighting

West Bank of the River Jordan - this area had been part of the Arab state of Jordan since the 1948-9 war; 750,000 people, mostly Palestinian Arabs, lived here (the population of Israel is about 2.5 million). Parts of the West Bank are very fertile, especially in the river valley

Sinai - a large area of Egyptian territory. It is mostly a desert. Very few people live here. On the western side is the Suez Canal and to the south east is the Gulf of Aqaba

Israeli conquests June 1967

The occupied territories

A SOURCE

The Israeli Defence Minister, General Dayan, said on the radio, after the capture of East Jerusalem:

We have unified Jerusalem, the divided capital of Israel. We have returned to the holiest of our holy places, never to part from it again.

B SOURCE

In August 1967, Arab leaders declared their main principles (from *The Middle East, 1914–1979*, T.G. Fraser, 1980):

No peace with Israel, no recognition of Israel, no negotiation with it. We insist on the rights of the Palestinian people in their country.

C SOURCE

In November 1967 the **United Nations** passed Resolution 242. As listed in *The Middle East, 1914–1979*, T.G. Fraser, 1980. This called for:

a) The withdrawal of Israeli armed forces from the territories occupied in the recent conflict.

b) Respect for the right of every state in the area to live in peace within secure and recognised boundaries, free from threats or acts of force.

Questions

a Give one reason why the Israelis were determined to keep control of Jerusalem.

b Why was Israel so successful in the Six-Day War?

c What were the effects of defeat on the Arabs?

d Use Sources A and B and your own knowledge to explain the problems of enforcing the UN Resolution 242 (Source C).

Study the map above and the information about the conquered territories that is given at the sides of the map. Make notes to explain what Israel had gained by capturing each of the territories:
- Golan Heights
- West Bank
- Sinai
- Gaza Strip.

Key Issues

- Why did Egypt and Syria attack Israel in 1973?
- Was this the Arabs' first 'victory' over Israel?

The Arabs are a proud people, yet they had been humiliated in the Six-Day War. They longed to regain their honour and their pride. Only by defeating Israel could they do this.

At the end of the Six-Day War, there was no peace treaty. In fact, fighting broke out again between Israel and Egypt in 1968. The Egyptians wished to clear the Suez Canal of sunken ships. The Israelis would only agree to this if their ships were allowed through the Canal. Over the next two years there were many clashes across the Canal. Both Egypt and Israel lost many men and weapons. By 1970 both sides were tiring. Nasser had not received the support he had hoped for from other Arab states. He appeared willing to recognise Israel. Then, in September 1970, he died. He had played an important part in world affairs for nearly twenty years.

Anwar Sadat took over as President of Egypt. Like Nasser, he was an army officer. He promised his people that the year 1971 'would not end without the conflict with Israel having been settled'.

There was still great tension on the Suez Canal. Neither side could use the Canal although both sides wanted to, and it seemed that fighting could flare up at any time. Egypt had to keep nearly one million men ready to fight and this was very expensive. It needed peace in order to clear the Canal and rebuild its cities. But Egypt also wanted to win back Sinai, the land east of the Suez Canal which it had lost in 1967.

NO PEACE, NO WAR

Sadat was prepared to recognise the state of Israel in order to regain the lost land. However, the Israelis were unwilling to discuss it and Sadat knew he could not defeat Israel in war. He therefore tried to get help from the United States to force Israel to give way. The United States was very friendly with Israel, but Sadat knew the US government wanted peace and friendship with the Arab states in the Middle East. As an Arab, Sadat hoped he could persuade the US government to use its influence with the Israelis. He sacked the members of his government who were anti-American. The United States, however, was too busy with the war in Vietnam. Besides, the 6 million Jews in America would oppose any attempt by the US government to 'bully' the Israelis. So the year 1971 ended, as it had begun, with 'no peace, no war'.

President Sadat of Egypt. He promised to settle the conflict with Israel.

EGYPT AND SYRIA PREPARE FOR WAR

Sadat then tried to obtain support from the Russians but, in return for supplying arms to Egypt, they wanted more control in Egyptian affairs. The Egyptian government could not stand any more Russian interference and so, in 1972, Sadat expelled all 15,000 Russian advisers who had been training Egypt's armed forces. This still made little difference to the United States' attitude.

However, Sadat now had strong financial support from the oil-rich state of Saudi Arabia. Also, the new Syrian leader, President Assad, became a close ally. Both Sadat and Assad realised that they would have to act soon if they were to recover Sinai and the Golan Heights, the lands they had lost in 1967. The Israelis were increasing their control of these areas: they were building new Jewish **settlements** and kept many troops there. Secretly, the Egyptian and Syrian leaders prepared for war. In September, Sadat made a defiant speech in Cairo:

*The United States is still under **Zionist** pressure and is wearing Zionist spectacles. The United States will have to take off those spectacles before they talk to us. We have had enough talk. We know our goal and we are determined to attain it.*

Very few people took his speech seriously. They had heard it all before. So had the Israelis. They had a low opinion of the Arab armies anyway. They were in for a shock.

THE FIGHTING

On 6 October, Egypt and Syria attacked. It was **Yom Kippur**, a holiday and the holiest day of the Jewish year. This meant that many soldiers were on leave, Israeli radio was closed down and most of the nation had stopped work. The Israelis were caught completely by surprise. The Egyptians crossed the Suez Canal and took back part of Sinai from the Israelis. At the same time, 500 Syrian tanks overwhelmed Israeli forces on the Golan Heights. The Israeli air force **retaliated** but discovered that the Arabs had Russian surface-to-air missiles, which they used very effectively.

It took the Israeli army three days to become fully **mobilised**. However, by 12 October they had pushed the Syrians back and, on 15 October, they thrust across the Suez Canal and cut off the Egyptian third army (see map above).

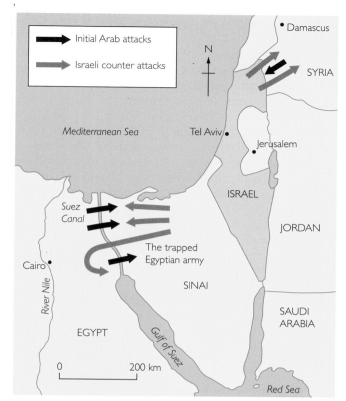

The Yom Kippur War, 1973.

THE OIL WAR

Two days after the Israelis crossed the Suez Canal and trapped a whole Egyptian army, the Arabs produced an unexpected weapon – oil. The West received much of its oil from the Middle East. The Arab oil-producing states decided to reduce oil production until the Israelis withdrew from the lands they had occupied in 1967. The richest oil state, Saudi Arabia, went further. It banned all oil exports to the United States and the Netherlands, the two countries which Saudi Arabia accused of helping the Israelis the most. The West was shocked.

What was the background to the Yom Kippur War of 1973? Make brief notes under the following headings:
- Tension over the Suez Canal
- Sadat seeks help from the USA and USSR
- Egypt's co-operation with Syria.

THE SUPERPOWERS STEP IN

The United States and USSR were deeply involved in the Yom Kippur War. The Russians sent arms to Egypt and Syria, and the United States sent them to Israel. When the Israelis crossed the Suez Canal, both **superpowers** stepped in. Russia advised Egypt to accept a ceasefire while it still held part of Sinai. The US government was worried by the Arab oil weapon, as many western countries depended on Arab oil. The United States also hoped to stop its ally, Israel, from attacking Cairo and Damascus (see map on page 31) for fear that Russian troops might be brought in.

Both superpowers were keen to be on good terms with each other at this time. American and Russian leaders met and together demanded a ceasefire, which the **United Nations** supported. The fighting ended on 24 October. A few days later, UN troops were sent to Egypt to preserve the ceasefire.

THE ARABS GAIN NEW CONFIDENCE

The Yom Kippur War was, in the end, a military victory for the Israelis. Yet again they had proved that their weapons, their training and their tactics were superior. But it was a political victory for the Arabs. They had completely surprised the Israelis and the rest of the world with their attack. They had proved that Arab soldiers could fight with courage and determination. Their leaders had shown skill. Above all, they had acted together, especially in the use of the oil weapon. As a result, the rest of the world showed much more respect for the Arabs.

One man, in particular, emerged from the war as a hero. Anwar Sadat had achieved exactly what he had set out to do. Firstly, he had broken the stalemate that existed before the war. Secondly, he had forced a change in US policy. The United States was to become far more friendly with the Arab states. A few years later, the American government was to play an important part in bringing about peace between Egypt and Israel.

A SOURCE

Egyptians storm across the Suez Canal, 1973. At the start of the war, 8000 troops crossed the Canal over ten bridges, by-passing the Israeli strong points. The whole operation had been planned and practised very thoroughly.

A cartoon from an American newspaper of October 1973, giving a US view of the conflict.

"Don't worry, Abdul, with this disguise the Americans won't let them shoot!"

C SOURCE

A historian writing about the results of the war (from *The Origins of the Arab-Israeli Wars*, R Ovendale, 2004).

Sadat emerged from the October War a world statesman, something Nasser had never achieved. Relations were established between Washington and Cairo. Sadat realised that only the US could effectively persuade Israel to make concessions in the **occupied territories**. *The United Nations decided on 'negotiations between the parties concerned aimed at establishing a just and lasting peace in the Middle East'.*

Questions

a How useful is Source A as evidence of Arab preparations for war?

b In what ways did the superpowers become involved in the Yom Kippur War?

c What was the importance of the 'oil weapon' in the outcome of the Yom Kippur War?

d 'The Yom Kippur War was a political and a military victory for the Arabs.' Use the sources and your own knowledge to explain whether you agree with this view.

e How was Israel able to survive four major wars against its Arab neighbours? You should refer in your answer to:
  • War of Independence, 1948–49
  • Suez War, 1956
  • Six-Day War, 1967
  • Yom Kippur War, 1973.

 THE PALESTINIAN REFUGEES

A refugee camp in Jordan, 1949.

WHERE DID THE REFUGEES GO?

During the fighting in 1948–49 between Israel and neighbouring Arab states, about 700,000 Arabs fled from their homes in Palestine. As you can see on the map below, most of them went to the West Bank or the Gaza Strip. Large numbers also went to Syria, Jordan and Lebanon. Today the **United Nations** reckons there are about 3 million Palestinian **refugees**.

THE UNITED NATIONS AND THE REFUGEES

After the 1948–49 war, the United Nations formed the UN Relief and Works Agency (**UNRWA**). This body set up camps for the refugees and provided food, clothing, shelter and education. At first, the refugees lived in tents as in the photograph on the right. The conditions are described on the page opposite, first by a British observer and then by a refugee himself, in Sources A and B.

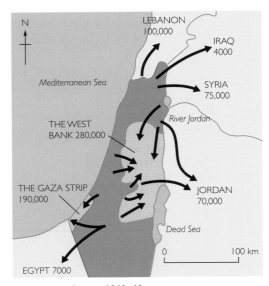

Palestinian refugees, 1948–49.

WHAT SOLUTIONS WERE THERE TO THE REFUGEE PROBLEM?

The Israelis refused to allow the refugees to return to their lands in Israel. The Israeli 'Law of Return' allows any Jew anywhere in the world to go and live in Israel but forbids Palestinians to do so. In 1967, on American television, the Israeli general, Moshe Dayan, explained:

We want to have a Jewish state. We can absorb the Arabs, but then it won't be the same country . . . We want a Jewish state like the French have a French state.

The Israelis were very willing to suggest a solution to the refugee problem as Source D shows – follow Israel's example!

But the views of the refugees were very different. They were Palestinians and they wanted to return to their homes in Palestine. Some, like Ghazi Daniel (Source E) were determined to fight for their country. Not all, however, were inspired to fight. Some were offered jobs in their new countries. Some migrated to other parts of the Middle East or the West. They became engineers, teachers, doctors or businessmen. A small number became very wealthy.

Nevertheless, most of the refugees remained poor and unemployed. Crowded together in the camps, they became frustrated and bitter. It was from the camps that the Palestine Liberation Organisation recruited most of its members.

A SOURCE

Jonathan Dimbleby, a British observer, comments in *The Palestinians*, 1979.

The conditions in the camps were atrocious. Families huddled bleakly in overcrowded tents. They were without adequate food or sanitation. When it rained, the narrow paths along each row were churned into mud which oozed into the tents. They lived in sodden clothes and slept in wet blankets. Influenza reached epidemic proportions. The young and old perished. Malnourished children were too weak to resist, and the old, left with no purpose, lacked the will.

B SOURCE

Ghazi Daniel, a refugee, remembers (from an account published by the PLO in 1972):

A few months after our arrival, we were penniless and had to move into a refugee camp with 2,000 other homeless Palestinians. It is beyond human endurance for a family of eleven to live in a small tent through all the seasons of the year on UNRWA rations. Fathers buried their children who died of hunger. Some buried their fathers who died of disease. On winter days we all crawled together to gain the warmth of humans . . .

C SOURCE

General Burns, a UN Commander, describes the conditions in the camps in Gaza in the 1950s:

They live in little huts of mud and concrete blocks, corrugated iron roofs, row after row. Fairly adequate medical service is provided, probably better than was enjoyed before they were expelled from their native villages.

Children swarm everywhere. There are primary schools for nearly all of them. There are secondary schools for many of the adolescents. And what will these youths and girls do when they have finished their secondary school training? There is no employment for them in the Strip, and very few can leave it to work elsewhere. The Gaza Strip resembles a vast concentration camp.

They can look to the east and see wide fields, once Arab land, cultivated extensively by a few Israelis.

D SOURCE

Abba Eban, Israeli ambassador to the United Nations, offers his solution to the refugee problem, in 1958:

Israel with her small territory, her poor water resources and her lack of money, has found homes, work and citizenship in the past ten years for nearly a million newcomers . . .

If Israel in these conditions could absorb nearly one million refugees – 450,000 of them from Arab lands – how much more easily could the vast Arab world find a home for a similar number of refugees?

E SOURCE

Ghazi Daniel, who was quoted in Source B, had strong views (from an account published by the PLO in 1972):

I am 24 years old. I was born in Nazareth but today I have no country . . . The two most precious ideals of my people are to remain Palestinians and not be refugees. These can only be realised if we return to our country and our homes . . . I am left with no alternative but to fight our enemy.

Questions

a   Give one reason why Israel would not allow Palestinians to return to their homes in Israel.
b   Describe the key features of the Palestinian refugee camps.
c   How useful is Source C for a historian studying the conditions in the refugee camps?
d   Sources D and E give different views of how to solve the refugee problem. Why do you think they are different?
e   Using all the sources and your own knowledge, explain why some of the refugees might decide to become **fedayeen**, or fighters, for the Palestinian cause.

13 THE PALESTINE LIBERATION ORGANISATION

Key Issue

- Why did some Palestinians become terrorists?

One of the hooded Palestinian terrorists on the balcony of the building where the Israeli athletes were held hostage during the Munich Olympics in 1972.

TERROR AT THE OLYMPICS, 1972

The image of the hooded gunman was many people's picture of a terrorist in the 1970s. It was certainly the image that many had of the Palestine Liberation Organisation (**PLO**). The man in the photograph and eight other Palestinians seized and killed eleven Israeli athletes at the Olympic Games in 1972.

This was not the first time that Arabs or Israelis had carried out what we call terrorist attacks. For example, in 1948, Jewish **extremists** killed the inhabitants of the Arab village of Deir Yassin (see Chapter 5). In the 1950s and 1960s, Palestinian **guerrillas** carried out many raids against Israeli villages. But after the Six-Day War, the terrorism spread to Europe and western newspapers reported it in full. In order to understand why this happened we need to study the PLO.

THE ORIGINS OF THE PLO

The PLO was set up in 1964. Its aim was to unite all Palestinians in the struggle to win back their land.

The largest group within the PLO was **Fatah** (see page 24), which had been set up by Yasser Arafat. From 1965 to 1967, Fatah carried out an increasing number of guerrilla attacks on Israel and was supported by the Arab states which bordered Israel. However, after the Six-Day War of 1967, things were to be very different for the PLO.

WHY WAS THE SIX-DAY WAR A TURNING POINT FOR THE PLO?

Syria, Jordan and Egypt, which had provided vital support for the PLO, were weakened by their heavy losses in the war. At the same time, Egypt and Syria became far more concerned about the lands they had lost to Israel than about the Palestinian **refugees**. Many Palestinians were now convinced that they would have to fight for their homeland on their own. This was even more urgent now that all the original land of Palestine, including the West Bank and Gaza Strip, was under Israeli rule.

When the West Bank was captured by the Israelis, 350,000 Palestinians fled. Most of the refugees went to Jordan. As a result, Fatah now concentrated its forces in Jordan. Fatah and other groups within the PLO started to recruit far more volunteers in the refugee camps. Ghazi Daniel was one of many Palestinian refugees for whom 1967 was a turning point:

The aggressive war of 1967 was a landmark in my life. The new expansion of Israel and the new waves of refugees multiplied the tragedy many times. This is why I have joined the Palestine Liberation Movement. We shall fight for the Palestinians' return.

Fatah now increased its raids into Israel. In retaliation, in 1968, the Israelis crossed the border into Jordan and launched a full-scale attack on a major Fatah base in Karameh. Although the Israelis destroyed the Palestinian base, the Palestinian forces (with the aid of Jordanian troops) knocked out several Israeli tanks and planes, and killed 28 Israeli troops. This inspired thousands of Palestinians to join the Palestinian armed forces. Between 1967 and 1970, Fatah forces killed over 500 Israelis. This was almost as many as the Israelis had lost in the whole Six-Day War.

Young Palestinian fighters.

ARAFAT BECOMES LEADER OF THE PLO

In 1968 Yasser Arafat became chairman of the PLO. He tried to co-ordinate the guerrilla activities of the various groups within the organisation. Like most of the PLO leaders, he wanted to limit the raids and the bombings to Israeli territory and Israeli targets because their military aim was strictly war on Israel. However, some extremist Palestinian groups caused divisions inside the PLO by carrying out attacks in other parts of the world. They pointed out that raids into Israel had achieved very little. They were impatient. They were not prepared to wait ten or twenty years to regain their country.

Yasser Arafat was born in Jerusalem in 1929. He was the founder of the Fatah organisation and became chairman of the PLO in 1968. For reasons of security, he slept in a different bed every night.

Make brief notes to answer the following questions:
- Why was the Six-Day War a turning point for the Palestinians?
- Why did many young Palestinians decide to join the PLO armed forces in the late 1960s?
- What was the main reason for splits developing within the PLO?

HIJACKS AND HOSTAGES

In December 1968, two Palestinians hijacked an Israeli passenger plane at Athens airport, killing one man. The Israelis **retaliated** by destroying thirteen aircraft in an attack on Beirut Airport in Lebanon, which is where the hijackers had come from. In the following years, there were many hijackings, kidnappings and bombings in Europe and elsewhere. At first, the targets were Israeli planes, embassies and offices, but some targets had very little to do with Israel at all (as you can see in the photograph below). The Israelis usually responded by bombing Palestinian bases in Lebanon, Jordan and Syria. Often these bases were near refugee camps so that hundreds of innocent Palestinians died. These Israeli **reprisals** received far less publicity in the western press than the Palestinian attacks.

THE PLO ARE EXPELLED FROM JORDAN, 1970

Sometimes terrorist violence led Arab to fight Arab. In Jordan, King Hussein feared the Israeli reprisals which followed Palestinian attacks that were launched from his country. In 1968 his troops had helped the Palestinians to inflict heavy casualties on the Israelis at Karameh. However, in September 1970, he decided he did not want any more raids launched on Israel from inside Jordan. Besides, the PLO were acting as if they ruled much of Jordan. So he ordered the Palestinians to obey him and his army.

Then, in the same month, four aircraft were hijacked by Palestinian extremists and three of the planes (belonging to British Airways, Swissair and TWA) were taken to a Palestinian base in Jordan. The passengers were set free but the British plane was blown up (see below). This made King Hussein fear foreign intervention and he was forced to act.

He ordered his army to take control of the PLO bases. The Palestinians resisted and, in the next ten days, nearly 10,000 of them were killed. The PLO offices in Jordan were shut down and their newspapers banned. The remaining guerrillas went to Syria and Lebanon.

BLACK SEPTEMBER

Palestinian extremists later got their revenge by murdering the Jordanian Prime Minister while he was in Egypt. The killers were members of a group called Black September, named after the month in which the Palestinian bases in Jordan were wiped out. Soon they began sending letter bombs to Israeli embassies in Europe.

Then, on 5 September 1972, they stunned the whole world. They attacked the Israeli athletes who were competing in the Olympic Games in Germany.

A newspaper headline on the Olympic murders.

The British plane, which was hijacked by Palestinians, is blown up in Jordan, September 1970

They killed two athletes and then demanded the release of 200 Palestinians in prison in Israel. When German police attempted a rescue, the Palestinians killed nine more athletes. The Palestinians got the massive publicity they wanted for their cause but not the release of their comrades. A few days later, the Israelis took their revenge and carried out reprisal raids on Syria and Lebanon, in which over 200 refugees were killed.

THE EFFECTS ON WORLD OPINION

Acts of terrorism made the Palestinians unpopular in the rest of the world. People were shocked by such brutal deeds. They branded the PLO, as a whole, as terrorists. However, terrorist acts made many people in Europe and other parts of the world begin to think more about the Palestinian problem. They read about the crowded, unhealthy camps in which hundreds of thousands of refugees had lived for twenty years. They came to understand that the Palestinian people were the helpless victims of war and asked themselves whether the guerrillas were in fact terrorists or freedom fighters.

TERRORISTS OR FREEDOM FIGHTERS?

A SOURCE

George Habash, leader of a Palestinian extremist group, said (from *Dispossessed: The Ordeal of the Palestinians, 1917–80*, D Gilmour, 1980):

When we hijack a plane it has more effect than if we killed 100 Israelis in battle. For decades world public opinion has been neither for nor against the Palestinians. It simply ignored us. At least the world is talking about us now.

B SOURCE

In the early 1970s, Sami el-Karami, a Palestinian, said (from *Dispossessed: The Ordeal of the Palestinians, 1917–80*, D Gilmour, 1980):

*The non-violent methods are very beautiful and very easy, and we wish we could win with these methods. Our people do not carry machine guns and bombs because they enjoy killing. It is for us the last resort. For 22 years we have waited for the **United Nations** and the United States, for liberty, for freedom and democracy. There was no result. So this is our last resort.*

C SOURCE

A Palestinian student in Lebanon wrote to his parents in 1968 (from a pamphlet published by the Palestinian Liberation Movement, 1969):

For 20 years our people have been waiting for a just solution to the Palestinian problem. All that we got was charity and humiliation while others continue to live in our homes. I refuse to remain a refugee. I have decided to join the freedom fighters and I ask for your blessing.

D SOURCE

A Palestinian woman, quoted in *The Middle East*, by Walter Oppenheim, 1989, explained:

I am proud that my son did not die in this refugee camp. The foreign press come here and take pictures of us standing in queues to obtain food rations. This is no life. I am proud that my son died in action, fighting on our occupied soil. I am already preparing my eight-year-old for the day he can fight for freedom too.

E SOURCE

Shimon Peres, Israeli Minister of Defence, said in a speech in 1976 (from *The Arab–Israeli Wars*, C Herzog, 1982):

Palestinian terrorist groups should be described in their true colours. They are impatient with democracy, undisciplined and dominated by murder and hatred.

Questions

a Give one reason why the athletes at Munich were chosen as a terrorist target.

b How useful is Source A for a historian studying why some Palestinians have used military force in order to achieve their objectives?

c Sources B and E give very different views about PLO bombings. Why do you think they are different?

d What did the PLO achieve by using terrorism? Use the sources and your own knowledge to explain your answer.

Key Issue

- Why did the Israelis invade Lebanon in 1978 and 1982?

On 10 April 1985, a sixteen-year-old Muslim girl, Sana M'Heidli, set off on a special mission. She drove a car packed with explosives towards a group of Israeli soldiers in Lebanon and then detonated the charge. She killed herself and two Israelis. We know it was a suicide mission because she explained what she was going to do on video beforehand. The photograph below comes from the video. It was later shown on television in Lebanon. What drove her to this desperate act? What were Israeli troops doing in Lebanon anyway?

CRISIS IN LEBANON

Until the 1970s, Lebanon was a fairly stable country and its capital, Beirut, was one of the richest cities in

Sana M'Heidli, sixteen-year-old suicide bomber. In her pre-recorded videotape, she said: 'I chose death in order to fulfil my national duty.' What do you think she meant?

the Middle East. However, in 1970, the **PLO** armed forces set up more bases there after they were expelled from Jordan (see page 38). They took over most of the south of Lebanon (some called it 'Fatahland') and frequently bombed villages in northern Israel. The Israelis hit back and, when they did so, Lebanese as well as Palestinians were killed.

In 1975 the Lebanese government ordered its army to regain control of the south. The Palestinians resisted and were helped by Lebanese Muslims. Most of the Lebanese army were Christian and soon there was a **civil war** between Christians and Muslims. Meanwhile, the PLO continued to carry out attacks on Israel from Lebanon. In 1978 a PLO suicide squad went further south and attacked a bus near Tel Aviv, killing 37 passengers.

ISRAELI INVASIONS, 1978 AND 1982

Three days after the bus bombing in 1978, Israeli troops invaded Lebanon. They seized the south of the country but the PLO forces melted away. The Israelis withdrew, under pressure from the United States, and **United Nations** troops were sent to keep the peace on the Lebanese–Israeli border.

Four years later, in June 1982, a group of Palestinians attempted to murder the Israeli ambassador in London. The Israelis again rolled across the Lebanese border. This time they had 170,000 troops, 3,500 tanks and 600 fighter planes. The UN peace-keeping forces were powerless to stop them. The Israelis were more successful in destroying PLO forces than they had been in 1978. However, thousands of Palestinian and Lebanese civilians were killed in the process and hundreds of thousands were made homeless.

The Israelis claimed that their aim was to drive out the Palestinian forces and destroy their bases. However, it soon became obvious that this was a full-scale invasion because the Israelis advanced north and surrounded the capital, Beirut. On one day alone, in August 1982, 127 air raids were launched on the city. The Israelis started shelling positions in the city that were held by the PLO. These positions were often in crowded residential areas so thousands more civilians were killed.

In mid-August, the United States intervened and the Israelis stopped shelling the city. American, French and Italian troops were sent out to supervise the evacuation of PLO guerrillas. Over 14,000 of them left Beirut to travel to other Arab states. Yasser Arafat moved his headquarters to Tunisia.

THE ISRAELIS WITHDRAW, 1985

When the PLO forces left Beirut, the Israelis withdrew their troops from the capital but they stayed in the south of Lebanon. The Israelis had succeeded in driving out the Palestinian armed forces but they had made many enemies amongst the Lebanese, especially the Muslims, in the south. Furthermore, they could still not be sure that they had driven out all the Palestinian forces. The **guerrillas** could easily hide in the huge, crowded **refugee** camps in Lebanon.

The Israeli government faced further problems. International opinion blamed the Israelis for thousands of civilian deaths. In Israel itself, huge numbers demonstrated against the war. They accused the government of turning a defensive war into an aggressive one and of sending hundreds of Israelis, as well as thousands of Palestinians and Lebanese, to their deaths unnecessarily.

Over the next two years, Israeli troops in the south of Lebanon were regularly attacked. When Israelis heard news of events like Sana M'Heidli's attack on their troops, many of them demanded a complete withdrawal from Lebanon. In 1985, the last Israeli troops finally left Lebanon. This was the longest war Israel had fought. Many regarded it as its first defeat.

Twenty years later, in 2006, Israel again launched attacks on Lebanon and bombed Beirut. You will read more of this in Chapter 22.

A SOURCE

Jacobo Timerman, an Israeli, wrote in *The Longest War*, 1982.

*The Israeli soldiers brought back with them stories about children completely different from the rocket-launching children who were the only ones mentioned by official Israeli **propaganda**. Lost children of ten or twelve caring for their younger brothers. They met Palestinian youths who served as volunteers in hospitals, who have friends, who want to have children some day, and who, like the Israelis, dream of a motorcycle, a girl . . .*

A PLO commander told me he had decided that the era of armed struggle was over and that Palestinians should pursue their aims using political, not military, methods. After 18 years of fighting, the PLO commander says 'Another death, whether Israeli or Palestinian, will not solve the problem. On the contrary, it will just make another family unhappy.'

B SOURCE

Israeli opponents of the war in Lebanon, 1982. Begin was the Prime Minister and Sharon was the Defence Minister in the Israeli government. Raful was the military commander.

Questions

a Why did Israeli forces invade Lebanon in 1978 and, again, in 1982?

b Explain what Source B tells about Israeli opposition to the war in Lebanon.

c How useful is Source A as evidence of changing attitudes amongst both Israeli and Palestinian military forces?

Key Issue

- What did the PLO, Israel and Egypt achieve by peaceful means?

Arafat speaking to the UN, 1974.

For 30 years, not one of the Arab states was willing to recognise Israel. Then, in the 1970s, came a breakthrough. After the Yom Kippur War of 1973, Egypt and Syria were still determined to win back the lands they had lost in 1967. But the Egyptians, unlike the Syrians, seemed willing to recognise the state of Israel, although they did not admit this in public.

Similarly, Yasser Arafat and some of the **PLO** leaders sounded more moderate. They hinted that they were ready to consider a 'mini-state' for the Palestinians – consisting of the West Bank and Gaza, where the majority of the inhabitants were Palestinian. In other words, the PLO moderates were no longer determined to remove the state of Israel.

THE GUN AND THE OLIVE BRANCH – ARAFAT AT THE UN

The PLO set up offices in many countries in order to win the support of foreign governments. At the end of 1974, Yasser Arafat was invited to speak at the **United Nations** for the first time. He told his audience:

*The roots of the Palestinian question are not the result of a conflict between two religions or two nationalisms. Neither is it a border conflict between two neighbouring states. It is the cause of a people deprived of its homeland, dispersed and uprooted, and living mostly in exile and in **refugee** camps.*

Many of Arafat's listeners at the UN were sympathetic. Some world leaders were beginning to admit that the Palestinians deserved a homeland. They also realised that if the Palestinians could be granted a homeland, then permanent peace in the Middle East was possible.

OPPOSITION TO ARAFAT

Although Arafat received a sympathetic hearing at the United Nations, he had many enemies elsewhere. The Israelis were furious with the United Nations for inviting Arafat to speak. They said the PLO was a 'murder organisation'. They refused to discuss the idea of a separate Palestinian state, however small it might be. They feared that the Palestinians aimed to take back all of Israel and would not be content with a small state next door to Israel.

The PLO was itself divided. Some **extremists** still insisted that Israel should be completely destroyed and taken over by Palestinians. They rejected the idea of a Palestinian 'mini-state' and did not want any Arab state to recognise Israel. In the mid-1970s they launched terrorist attacks both inside Israel and in other parts of the world.

SADAT FLIES TO ISRAEL, 1977

After the Yom Kippur War in 1973, the US government worked hard to bring peace to the Middle East. The Americans persuaded the Israelis and the Egyptians to draw back their forces on the Suez Canal in January 1974. In March, Saudi Arabia started selling oil to the United States again. The following year, the Suez Canal was reopened and the Israeli and Egyptian forces drew back on the Sinai front also. A United Nations force kept the two sides apart.

The bravest peacemaker was undoubtedly President Sadat of Egypt. He wanted permanent peace because four wars against Israel had cost many lives and much money. Egypt needed a lasting peace in order to recover. In 1977 Sadat surprised the world by announcing that he was willing to go to Israel and discuss peace. This was a bold move: for 30 years Arab leaders had refused even to accept Israel's existence. Ten days later he flew to Israel.

The following month, the Israeli Prime Minister, Menachem Begin, went to Egypt and peace talks were started. When they slowed down in 1978, US President Carter invited the Egyptian and Israeli leaders to Camp David in the United States. For thirteen days, the three men and their advisers discussed a peace settlement.

THE CAMP DAVID AGREEMENTS OF 1978

At Camp David, a framework for peace between Israel and Egypt was agreed. The main points were:

- Israeli forces to be withdrawn from Sinai
- Egypt to regain all of Sinai within three years
- Israeli shipping to have free passage through the Suez Canal and the Straits of Tiran (see map on page 29).

Six months after Camp David, in March 1979, the Egyptian and Israeli leaders signed a peace treaty which confirmed what they had agreed at Camp David. Both sides finally agreed to recognise 'each other's right to live in peace within their secure and recognised boundaries'.

The signing of the Egypt–Israel peace treaty was a great breakthrough in Arab–Israeli relations. However, the Palestinian problem still remained at the heart of the conflict in the Middle East. A solution seemed as far off as ever.

The Israeli and Egyptian leaders shake hands after Camp David while US President Carter looks on, 1978.

A SOURCE

Arafat gave his speech to the UN with a holster attached to his hip, although he left the gun outside the hall. He ended the speech with the words:

Today I have come bearing an olive branch [a symbol of peace] and a freedom fighter's gun. Do not let the olive branch fall from my hand.

B SOURCE

On 20 November 1977, Sadat spoke to the Israeli parliament:

We used to reject you, and we had our reasons and grievances. But I say to you today and I say to the whole world that we accept that we should live with you in lasting and just peace.

C SOURCE

In his reply, the Israeli Prime Minister said:

The time of the flight from Cairo to Jerusalem is short but the distance until last night was almost infinite.

Questions

a How useful is Source A to a historian studying Arafat's speech at the UN?

b How important do you think the speeches (Sources B and C) were in leading to the Camp David Agreement?

c Did the Palestinians achieve more by terror or by peaceful means from 1964 to 1974? You will need to re-read Chapter 13 in order to answer this question. You may use the following information to help you with your answer:
- 1964: the formation of the PLO
- raids into Israel by **Fatah**
- 1972: the Munich Olympics
- 1974: Arafat's speech at the UN.

16 THE ROLE OF THE SUPERPOWERS

Key Issue

- What part did the United States and the USSR play in the Arab–Israeli conflict?

THE SIX-DAY WAR, 1967

As you learnt in Chapter 10, the Six-Day War was an overwhelming victory for the Israelis. Israel's Arab opponents, especially Egypt and Syria, were devastated. However, the USSR immediately began to re-equip Egypt and Syria, while the United States provided more weapons for Israel's armed forces.

THE YOM KIPPUR WAR, 1973

In the Yom Kippur War of 1973, both the superpowers poured arms into the conflict in order to support their allies. The superpowers also played a big part in ending the war. Both sides wanted to avoid being dragged into the fighting and had their own reasons for wanting to ease the tension in the Cold War. (You can read how the superpowers brought about a ceasefire on page 32.)

The Arab use of the 'oil weapon' in the Yom Kippur War shocked the Americans and, over the next few years, the United States government did much to improve its relations with the Arab world and to bring peace to the region. In 1978, the US President, Jimmy Carter, brought the Israeli and Egyptian leaders together at Camp David and, a year later, the Egypt–Israel peace treaty was signed (see page 43). The United States now began to supply money and weapons to Egypt as well as to Israel.

The cartoon opposite (Source A) shows the United States and the USSR pouring arms into the 'boiling pot' of the Middle East. This chapter will examine how and why the two superpowers became involved in the conflict.

The United States, with its large and influential Jewish population, played a major part in the creation of the Jewish state of Israel (as you saw in Chapter 4). The USSR also supported the new state at that time because it believed that the Jews needed a state of their own.

Then, in the 1950s, the USSR responded to Egypt's request for weapons. With the Cold War between the United States and the USSR developing, the Russians saw a great opportunity to win allies, and to balance America's influence in the Middle East.

THE SUPERPOWERS AND THE SUEZ WAR, 1956

In the Suez War of 1956, both the USSR and the United States condemned Anglo-French military action against Egypt (see Chapters 7 and 8) and thus speeded up an end to the fighting. However, it was the Russians who gained most. Egypt and Syria looked to the USSR for the aid they needed and the USSR responded, both with weapons and military advisers.

Similarly, the United States continued to arm Israel. In fact, the United States gave billions of dollars of financial aid and weapons to Israel (and still does today). The United States felt that Israel was its only close, firm friend in the Middle East. And, of course, America's Jewish population put a lot of pressure on its government to support Israel (which it also still does today).

THE END OF THE COLD WAR

Towards the end of the 1980s, relations between the United States and the USSR improved. As the communist system of government crumbled and the USSR broke up, Russian influence in the Middle East faded. Countries like Syria could no longer rely on Russian arms and financial support. The United States no longer felt it *had* to support Israel in order to maintain its influence in the Middle East.

In 1991, the United States, the only remaining superpower, formed a multi-national military force to drive Iraqi troops out of Kuwait (see page 48). Even Russia and its former ally Syria supported the Americans. Later in the same year, the United States government put pressure on the Israelis (by holding back money and weapons) in order to get them to hold peace talks with the Palestinians. Two years later, Israel and the PLO signed a peace agreement. You will read more about this in Chapter 18.

SOURCE

A cartoon from the British magazine *Punch*, November 1967. The two figures in the cartoon represent Johnson and Brezhnev, the American and Russian leaders.

MIDDLE EAST

C **SOURCE**

On 11 October 1973, the *Daily Mail* reported:

Big Two send arms

THE MIDDLE EAST conflict took on a new dimension of danger last night as both Russia and America began airlifting fresh weapons to each side.

D **SOURCE**

From a British history book, *The Arab–Israeli Conflict*, Tony Rea and John Wright, 1997.

Carter's greatest triumph in foreign affairs came in 1978 when he worked out the framework for the peace treaty between Egypt and Israel, known as Camp David. President Sadat of Egypt paid tribute to Carter by insisting on only one signing of the treaty in Washington, USA, saying, 'Jimmy Carter has done it and the show is his show.'

B **SOURCE**

A blindfolded Russian military adviser is led away by Israeli troops during the Israeli advance into Syria in 1967.

Questions

a Between 1948 and 1997, the USA gave Israel $85 billion in aid. Why has the USA given such large amounts of aid to Israel?

b How useful is Source A for an understanding of superpower involvement in the Arab–Israeli conflict?

c To what extent do Sources B and C support the evidence of Source A about superpower involvement in the Middle East?

d Have the USA and Russia helped or hindered in the search for peace between the Arabs and Israel since 1948? You should refer in your answer to:
   • supply of arms to Israel and the Arab states
   • ending the fighting over Suez in 1956
   • bringing about a ceasefire in the Yom Kippur War, 1973
   • US role in peacemaking in 1978 and 1991–93 (see Chapter 18).

17 THE PALESTINIAN INTIFADA, 1987–93

Key Issue

- Why did a Palestinian uprising break out in the occupied territories in 1987?

On 8 December 1987, an Israeli army vehicle in Gaza crashed into a lorry, killing four of the Palestinians on board. Rumours spread that it had been a deliberate act of revenge for the killing of an Israeli two days before. The funerals of the Palestinians became huge demonstrations. At one of them, a youth was shot dead by an Israeli soldier. As tension mounted, thousands of Palestinians took to the streets, both in Gaza and on the West Bank, and put up barricades of tyres, corrugated iron and building materials. From behind them, they stoned Israeli army patrols. What was the background to this uprising or '**Intifada**'?

LIFE IN THE OCCUPIED TERRITORIES

Since 1967, thousands of Israeli troops had been stationed in Gaza and the West Bank. They rounded up PLO suspects and others whom they saw as a threat to their security. Many were either jailed or deported (usually to Jordan). Sometimes their houses were blown up, leaving their families homeless.

The Israeli army also confiscated land for the building of Jewish **settlements**. These were built for security reasons, to keep an eye on the Palestinians. They also built roads, to link the towns and settlements, and military camps and checkpoints.

It became a common sight for the Palestinians to see Jewish settlements being built on land they considered to be theirs. By 1987, there were over 80,000 Jews living in settlements in and around Jerusalem and another 20,000 living in parts of the West Bank and in Gaza. The Intifada may have been triggered by a single incident, but years of living under Israeli occupation had led to increasing hatred and tension.

Young Palestinians hurl stones at Israeli soldiers in Gaza, 1987.

THE ISRAELI RESPONSE TO THE INTIFADA

The Intifada took everyone by surprise – Israel, the PLO, the Arab states and the rest of the world. Not surprisingly, the Israeli government insisted on an 'iron fist' policy. Live ammunition was used. Newspapers and television around the world showed teenagers being shot by Israeli troops. This led the Israeli government to announce that it would no longer use bullets. Instead, a policy of 'might, power and beatings' would be adopted. But still the death toll rose and worldwide publicity was given to the tear-gassing of demonstrators, the beatings of youths, the closing of schools and colleges. By September 1988, 346 Palestinians had been killed. Many of them were under sixteen.

EFFECTS OF THE INTIFADA

Almost every Palestinian family living in the **occupied territories** was affected by the Intifada. So were many Israeli families because thousands of soldiers, whether regular troops or **reservists**, were called up to do **military service** on the West Bank or in Gaza. The following extracts were all taken from interviews conducted in the years after the Intifada began.

A SOURCE

Ali, aged 23, was living in a **refugee** camp on the West Bank (from *Justice and the Intifada*, K Bergen, 1991):

Before the Intifada began, we, the Palestinian people, were already convinced of the justice of our struggle. For the rest of the world, other problems were more important. But because of the Intifada, the entire world has now been able to see what is happening in this land. Now some nations see the nature of the occupation here and see the Palestinian people demanding their rights, demanding a state.

B SOURCE

Amnon, an Israeli who was on military service in Gaza (from *Justice and the Intifada*, K Bergen, 1991):

I didn't understand why they hate me. I spoke to one Palestinian girl. I told her I don't hate her. She said she hates us. She sees us all as Nazis. Someone tried to kill me. He stood above me with a rock. He was on the roof and I pointed my gun at him and told him in Arabic that I would shoot him. He said 'Shoot me, I don't care.' He aimed and threw the rock at me. I jumped to one side, escaping the stone.

C SOURCE

Umm Assad, a Palestinian woman who was living in a refugee camp in Gaza (from *Justice and the Intifada*, K Bergen, 1991):

At one o'clock in the morning the Israeli soldiers came. They took one son who was studying at the university. They said he was doing bad things. They demanded a fine. We gave them the money but he was still tried and imprisoned. Then they came again and took another son who had been wounded. He was sleeping in his bed. Again they came in the middle of the night, not during the day. The boy wanted to go to university, to go abroad to study, and instead they came and took him. He has been in prison for fifteen months. We are not well off, yet we paid their fines; life has to go on. But meanwhile they continue to arrest the youth, to kill them in the streets.

D SOURCE

Alon, an Israeli on military service on the West Bank (from *Justice and the Intifada*, K Bergen, 1991):

The soldiers caught a child. The commander arrived, he grabbed the child and told him: 'Climb up on the electrical pole' – it was a high-tension wire – 'and take down the PLO flag.' It was a huge pole, impossible to climb. He started and after a few meters he could not go on. The commander started to hit the child in the legs and told him to go on climbing. I was in shock but the soldiers were enjoying it. Then the father came out of the house and he started to cry: 'Leave my child alone, I'll take it down.' He started climbing. He was quite old and couldn't do it. And the commander started hitting him. I started to fight with the commander. He said: 'They put it there. They can take it down.' I asked: 'How will he get it down? It's impossible.' We were actually fighting in front of the soldiers, and finally he gave in. They did not bring down the flag.

Questions

a **What led to the outbreak of the Intifada and how did the Israeli government respond?**

b **How useful is Source A to a historian studying the Intifada?**

c **Describe the effects that the Intifada had on Palestinians and on Israeli soldiers.**

d **In what ways was the Intifada a battle that neither side could win? Use the sources and your own knowledge to answer this question.**

Key Issue

- How did Israel and the PLO make peace?

At the height of the **Intifada**, in December 1988, the United States opened secret talks with PLO officials. The Americans persuaded Yasser Arafat to do something he had never done before publicly: he rejected terrorism. Now, at last, the United States was willing to negotiate openly with the PLO and to put more pressure on the Israelis to open peace talks with the Palestinians.

THE IRAQI INVASION OF KUWAIT, 1990

Before any peace talks between Israel and the Palestinians were started, another conflict in the Middle East grabbed the headlines. In August 1990, Iraqi troops invaded Kuwait, another Arab state. The Iraqis claimed that Kuwait belonged to them. Most of the Arab world, as well as other countries, condemned the Iraqi attack. The United States rushed troops to the Middle East. The **United Nations** called for Iraq to withdraw and the Americans led a huge multi-national force which, by the end of February 1991, had driven the Iraqis out of Kuwait. This was known as the Gulf War because Kuwait is on the Persian Gulf.

Palestinians and other Arabs were quick to point out what they saw as the United States' double standards. They said that the Americans had acted swiftly to enforce the UN demand for Iraq to withdraw from Kuwait yet they had not managed, even after twenty years, to persuade Israel to withdraw its troops from the **occupied territories** of Gaza and the West Bank. The UN had demanded this as far back as 1967.

The US government was stung by this criticism. It wanted to keep the support of Arab states like Egypt, Saudi Arabia, even Syria, who had joined the United States in the fight against Iraq. Also, America's allies in the West depended on imports of oil from Arab states. So the US government was at last willing to put more pressure on Israel. It was now in a better position to do so.

THE END OF THE COLD WAR

The reason for this change was that the **Cold War** (between the United States and the **USSR**) had now ended. The communist government in Russia was, by this time, collapsing. It was no longer supporting the Arab states so strongly. This meant that the United States no longer had to support Israel in order to contain a Russian threat in the Middle East. The US government could therefore push the Israelis into making peace. It threatened to hold back money and arms from Israel. In fact, the United States could actually co-operate with Russia because Russia was now desperate for US financial aid. This meant that the United States could also expect the co-operation of Arab leaders who would no longer be able to rely on Russia for arms and money.

THE MADRID CONFERENCE, 1991

In October 1991, the US government persuaded the Israelis to hold face-to-face talks with Palestinian leaders. By now, an increasing number of both Israelis and Palestinians were coming to the conclusion that they had more to gain from making peace than making war. These talks were held in Madrid. Little progress was made in the talks while the **extremists** on both sides attempted to disrupt the discussions by acts of violence.

THE BREAKTHROUGH: AGREEMENT IN OSLO, SEPTEMBER 1993

In 1993, discussions were started up again. This time they were held in secret, in Oslo, in neutral Norway, away from the glare of worldwide publicity. In June 1993, the Israeli people elected a new government, which promised to work for peace with the Palestinians. Finally, in September, after eight months of secret talks, the PLO leader, Yasser Arafat, and the head of the new Israeli government, Yitzhak Rabin, exchanged letters.

Arafat, in his letter, rejected the use of terrorism, called for an end to the Intifada and recognised 'the right of Israel to exist in peace and security'. He had never made such clear statements before. Rabin, in his letter, recognised 'the PLO as the representative of the Palestinian people'. In the past, the Israeli government had refused to believe that the PLO really represented the Palestinian people and had regarded it as just a terrorist organisation.

Rabin (left) and Arafat (right) shake hands while US President Clinton looks on, 1993.

PLO leader Yasser Arafat waves to Palestinians on his way into Gaza, July 1994. It was the first time he had set foot on Palestinian land for 27 years. Two years later, he was elected President of the Palestinian Authority.

THE 1993 PEACE AGREEMENT

On 13 September 1993, the two leaders signed an agreement. This paved the way for a step-by-step approach towards self-government for the Palestinians. Then, in front of all the world's cameras at the White House in Washington, Arafat and Rabin shook hands. It would have been almost impossible to imagine this happening a few years before. At last, a major break-through had been made in resolving the Palestinian problem, the problem of a people without a land.

WHAT WAS AGREED?

The Israeli and Palestinian leaders agreed that:

- Israeli troops would be withdrawn from Gaza and the city of Jericho (see map on page 57) on the West Bank. After that, they would be withdrawn from other parts, but not all, of the West Bank.
- Elections would be held for a Palestinian Authority (PA) to run the West Bank and Gaza for five years.
- During these five years, a final settlement would be discussed.

OSLO ACCORD, 1995

Two years later, in 1995, a second Israeli–Palestinian agreement was signed. It became known as the Oslo II Accord. It was agreed that:

- Elections to the Palestinian Authority would finally be held.
- Israeli forces would withdraw from major Palestinian towns.

- Palestinian prisoners would be released from Israeli jails.

ISRAEL–JORDAN PEACE TREATY, 1994

Following the Israeli–Palestinian agreement of 1993, Jordan signed a peace treaty with Israel in which the two sides settled their dispute over their borders. More importantly, Jordan became the second Arab state (after Egypt in 1978) to recognise the state of Israel and to open up trade and other links. Relations between Israel and Syria, however, remain very bitter and no agreement has been reached on the return of the Golan Heights (see page 29) to Syria.

Questions

a Why did the USA put more pressure on Israel to make peace with the PLO in the early 1990s?

b Why did Israel and the PLO sign peace accords in 1993 and 1995? You may use the following information to help you with your answer:
- 1987–93: the impact of the Intifada
- 1989: the end of the Cold War
- 1990: the Gulf War
- 1991–93: talks in Madrid and Oslo
- the roles of Arafat and Rabin.

Key Issue

- What were the issues to be decided before a final settlement could be agreed?

The Oslo peace agreements were intended to build confidence and trust between the Israelis and the Palestinians. This they did. The most difficult questions were to be discussed, over the five years from 1993 to 1998, before a final settlement could be agreed. These were the main issues:

1 **The future of Jerusalem** Both Israelis and Palestinians wanted it as their capital. The Israelis were determined to ensure that they continued to control all of the city and that it remained their capital. By the late 1990s, East Jerusalem, which was mostly Arab, was encircled by Israeli **settlements** containing 150,000 Israelis.

2 **Jewish settlements in the occupied territories** What would happen to the numerous Israeli settlements on the West Bank? Should they be given up? If not, should Israeli troops continue to guard those settlements and protect the Jewish inhabitants?

3 **An independent Palestinian state** Would most Palestinians agree to a state which was limited to the West Bank and Gaza or would many demand all of Palestine (meaning the end of Israel)? Even if a Palestinian state was limited to the West Bank and Gaza, Palestinians would surely want a completely independent state. Yet if Israeli troops stayed on the West Bank, then it would not be part of a completely independent Palestine, simply because Jewish (i.e. foreign) troops were stationed there. The Israelis, for their part, were worried about their security as the map (source E) shows. They suspected that many Palestinians would not be satisfied with a mini-state and that Israel would constantly face the threat of destruction.

'No going home?' A Palestinian refugee in Lebanon. In 1997, an Arab information service in Britain wrote: 'Keeping millions of Palestinians without a homeland will amount to leaving an unexploded bomb under any peace agreement signed.'

4 **The Palestinian refugees' right to return** Would the **refugees** in Lebanon, Syria, Jordan and other Arab countries be allowed to return to the homes they had left during the fighting in 1948–49? Most Israelis believed that the Palestinians should not be allowed to return. They thought that the Jews would be swamped if all the Palestinian refugees returned and the Palestinians might then form the majority of the population of Israel.

ATTITUDES TO THE PEACE PROCESS

The following sources all come from the 1990s.

A SOURCE

Faisal Husseini, a Palestinian writer and spokesman for the West Bank Palestinians:

We have decided to get rid of some of our grand dreams. Instead of having our state in all our homeland, we are realistic in deciding to accept a state in only part of our homeland, alongside the state of Israel.

B SOURCE

David Hammo, an Israeli, who was born in Morocco and came to Israel as a boy:

Eventually there will be a Palestinian state, and this has penetrated the dreams of every Israeli. Everyone knows it is inevitable, it is just a question of time.

C SOURCE

A Palestinian refugee in Lebanon said:

*I have 16 children, six of whom died as **martyrs**. My house was destroyed by the Israelis. We have made all these sacrifices and for what? For only Gaza and the West Bank? No, it's not big enough. Where is my home in Acre [in Israel]? We made sacrifices for the whole of Palestine, not for a small part.*

D SOURCE

Benny Katzover, an Israeli who lives in a Jewish settlement on the West Bank:

A Palestinian state will never be established. It cannot be established. No government in Israel, or anywhere else, can simply remove the 140,000 Jews who live in Judea and Samaria [the West Bank], the 160,000 Jews in East Jerusalem, or the 150 Jewish settlements.

E SOURCE

'The map that speaks louder than words'. This is adapted from a pamphlet produced by The Britain/Israel Public Affairs Centre.

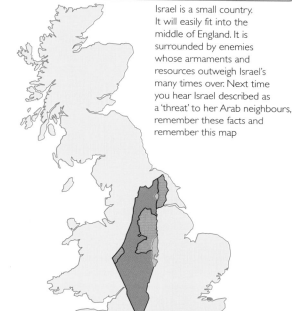

Israel is a small country. It will easily fit into the middle of England. It is surrounded by enemies whose armaments and resources outweigh Israel's many times over. Next time you hear Israel described as a 'threat' to her Arab neighbours, remember these facts and remember this map

Questions

a Sources A and C give different Palestinian views of the peace process. Why do you think they are different?
b How useful are Sources B and D for an understanding of Israeli attitudes towards a Palestinian state?
c Use Source E to explain why some Israelis oppose a Palestinian state.

Key Issue

- Why did the peace process slow down in the 1990s?

A SOURCE

A SOURCE

This cartoon appeared in the Guardian in May 1994 after the Israeli leader, Rabin, and the Palestinian leader, Arafat, had signed an agreement that allowed for the Palestinian Authority to recruit a maximum of 9000 police to work in Gaza and Jericho.

The 1993 and 1995 Oslo Accords, as the peace agreements were known, were greeted as a breakthrough right across the world. There was widespread confidence that the 'peace process' would lead to a final peaceful settlement of the Palestinian problem, the heart of the Middle East conflict.

ISRAELI AND PALESTINIAN VIEWS OF THE PEACE PROCESS

Despite the handshake on the White House lawn and the subsequent agreements, there was still deep distrust. Above all, there were very different views of what the peace agreements meant. For the Israelis, they meant that they would withdraw their troops from Gaza and some parts of the West Bank but still keep overall control. They still saw their troops having the main responsibility for security, both inside the West Bank and on its borders. After all, there were 200,000 Israeli settlers to protect. Also, the roads leading to the **settlements** and their water supplies had to be protected. All of this would require many troops.

By contrast, most of the Palestinians saw the peace agreement as the first step towards the establishment of an independent, Palestinian state. They saw the Palestinian Authority (PA) as the basis of a government which would lay the foundations for the new Palestinian state. The PA, however, was seen by most Israelis as a very limited form of self-government. For example, it might run schools and hospitals and set up a Palestinian police force to keep law and order amongst the Palestinian people. But the Israelis still saw themselves as remaining in overall control of security in Gaza and on the West Bank.

PEACEMAKING SLOWS DOWN

Over the next few years, the pace of change was too slow for most Palestinians. The withdrawal of Israeli troops from Palestinian towns was very gradual and, worst of all from a Palestinian perspective, the Israelis kept on building Jewish settlements in the **occupied territories**. This involved the seizure of Palestinian land and often the demolition of their homes. It also meant the building of roads (which cut through Palestinian areas) for Jewish-only use and it meant more wells sunk to provide water for Jewish-only settlements.

The building of more Jewish settlements had not been banned in the Oslo agreements but, in the eyes of the Palestinians, it went against the spirit of the agreements. It led to the takeover of more of their land. In their frustration and anger, many Palestinians switched their support from the **PLO** to more **militant** Palestinian groups. Amongst these groups was **HAMAS**, whose initials, in Arabic, stood for the Movement of the Islamic Revolution.

HAMAS AND SUICIDE BOMBING

HAMAS had opposed the so-called 'peace process' because they believed that the Palestinians gained little. For a start, there was no promise of an independent Palestinian state. Besides which, it was the declared aim of HAMAS to destroy the state of Israel. Support for HAMAS increased dramatically after a Jewish settler, Baruch Goldstein, went on the rampage and killed 29 Palestinians at a mosque in Hebron, on the West Bank, in 1994. Organisations like HAMAS blamed the Israeli government for not disarming the settlers and for allowing this to happen. Over the next few years, HAMAS embarked on a campaign of suicide bombings, both in Israel itself and in the occupied territories.

Bombings in turn made the Israeli government take a harder line. They blamed Arafat and the Palestinian Authority (PA) for not controlling the militants, and Israeli troops moved back into areas in Gaza and the West Bank which they had recently left. **Curfews** were imposed in the towns, cities and **refugee** camps, and the Israelis closed the border crossings between Israel and the occupied territories. They did this so as to seal their borders and prevent suicide bombers slipping through. But it also meant that Palestinians could not cross into Israel where many of them worked by day. This increased unemployment and hardship amongst the Palestinians. It also hurt the Israeli economy because many Israeli farms and factories depended on a plentiful supply of cheap Palestinian labour.

Despite these setbacks, talks between the Israeli government and Palestinian Authority were still held, often in neutral, foreign countries. Agreements were made to withdraw Israeli troops from Palestinian towns and cities on the West Bank and, in return, Arafat agreed to arrest HAMAS militants. But, time and time again, it was the **extremists** on both sides who dominated the headlines. And it was not always Jew versus Arab and Arab versus Jew, as you will see on the next page.

B SOURCE

A Palestinian woman argues with an Israeli soldier while being held at gunpoint in the West Bank town of Hebron. After clashes between Palestinians and Israeli security forces, the army imposed a curfew on the town in December 1996.

Questions

a In what ways did Israeli and Palestinian views of the peace process differ?

b How useful is the cartoon in Source A for an understanding of the Israeli–Palestinian peace process?

c Why did Palestinian support for HAMAS increase in the 1990s?

d What can you learn about the Israeli–Palestinian conflict in the 1990s from Source B?

Make brief notes on the breakdown of the peace process. Use the following headings:
- Israeli and Palestinian views of the Oslo agreements
- Jewish settlements
- Suicide bombings.

THE ASSASSINATION OF RABIN, NOVEMBER 1995

In November 1995, 150,000 Israelis gathered in Tel Aviv for a peace rally. The main speaker was the Prime Minister Yitzak Rabin, who had signed the peace deal in 1993. After the rally, a young Israeli, Yigal Amir, stepped up and shot him. Rabin died on the way to hospital. The assassin was a member of an Israeli group that opposed any peace with the Palestinians. This group believed that the West Bank (which they called Judea and Samaria, as in the Bible) was part of the Land of Israel, the land that God had promised to the Jews. In their view, Rabin had been prepared to give away parts of the sacred Land of Israel and was thus a traitor and an enemy of the Jewish people. At his trial, Amir said: 'When I shot Rabin, I felt I was shooting a terrorist.'

The majority of Israelis supported the 'peace process'. They believed that it was worth exchanging land for security and accepted that, one day, there would have to be a Palestinian state based on the West

Noa Ben Artzi weeps as she addresses the funeral service for her grandfather Yitzhak Rabin, November 1995.

C SOURCE

An Israeli bulldozer prepares to flatten an Arab house on the West Bank, February 1997, to make way for a larger Jewish settlement.

Bank and Gaza. But, after a series of suicide bombings on crowded buses in Israeli towns, the hardliners gained more support. In May 1996, six months after the death of Rabin, a new government was elected in Israel. This government opposed any further negotiations with Arafat and the Palestinian Authority.

BUILDING NEW JEWISH SETTLEMENTS

In February 1997, the new Israeli government gave the go-ahead to the building of 6500 new homes on Arab land in East Jerusalem. This would complete a chain of Jewish settlements round the eastern side of Jerusalem and effectively cut off the Arab inhabitants of East Jerusalem from the rest of the West Bank (see map on page 57). This further dashed Palestinian hopes of making East Jerusalem the capital of an independent state of Palestine.

As the bulldozers went into action to clear the ground for building to start, the new Israeli Prime Minister announced: 'The battle for Jerusalem has begun.' A Palestinian leader retorted: 'Israel's bulldozers have destroyed any chance for peace'.

D SOURCE

A report in the *Guardian* newspaper, 31 July 1997.

Horror in the market place
Israel stunned as 15 die in suicide bombing, shattering peace hopes
The bombers dressed in black. They wore suits and ties and carried briefcases. They parked their car a few hundred yards from Jerusalem's market and walked into the dense mix of fruit, vegetables and heaving crowds. The two men were almost certainly in sight of one another when they pulled the cords on their twin bombs.

By late last night, the toll was 15 dead and more than 150 wounded. All Palestinians working in Israel were ordered back to the West Bank and Gaza, which have been sealed off.

Yasser Arafat, the Palestinian leader, declared a state of emergency yesterday in the territories controlled by his Palestinian Authority and began arresting Islamic militants. Leaflets circulating in Palestinian areas claimed the attack had been carried out by the main Palestinian extremist group, HAMAS.

'I condemn completely this terrorist act because it is against the peace process, against the Palestinians and against the Israelis,' said Arafat.

E SOURCE

This cartoon was published in *The Times* the day after the suicide bombing reported in Source B. HAMAS claimed that the attack was retaliation for a poster, put up by a settler in a West Bank town, which showed the Muslim prophet Mohammed as a pig. This was deeply offensive to Muslims who see the pig as unclean.

Questions

a Why was the Israeli Prime Minister Yitzak Rabin assassinated in 1995?
b Why do you think the Israeli government supported the building of more Jewish settlements?
c What does Source C tell you about Israeli policy in the occupied territories?
d How useful is Source D for a historian studying Palestinian terrorism?
e Study Source E. The drawing on the head scarf is of Yasser Arafat. What comment is the cartoonist making on the bombings reported in Source D?

21 THE SECOND INTIFADA, 2000–05

Key Issue

- What have been the obstacles to peace in the twenty-first century?

On 28 September 2000, the Israeli leader, Ariel Sharon, made a tour of Jerusalem's Temple Mount, the site of a holy Muslim shrine. He obviously expected to cause trouble as he was accompanied by over a thousand police! And he certainly got it. The visit was seen as highly provocative by Palestinians. Many saw it as a threat to impose Israeli control over the holy sites. Whatever the intentions, demonstrations followed and Israeli troops shot seven Palestinians and wounded over 200. This marked the start of a second **Intifada** (or uprising) and, within a month, 127 Palestinians had been killed.

THE ORIGINS OF THE SECOND INTIFADA

The underlying cause of the second Intifada was the frustration and anger of the Palestinians in the **occupied territories** of the West Bank and in Gaza. Seven years after the Oslo peace agreement of 1993, little progress had been made in the 'peace process'. For many, both in Israel and on the West Bank and in Gaza, things had worsened: the Palestinian suicide bombings, the Israeli **reprisals** and the building of more Jewish **settlements** continued. The Palestinians, in particular, felt that they were hemmed in.

- In **Gaza,** which is smaller than the Isle of Wight, there were a million Palestinians, half of them in **refugee** camps and dependent on UN hand-outs, living on a thin strip of land between the sea and the Israeli border. There were only a few thousand Jewish settlers but they and the troops protecting them controlled a third of the land and most of the water supplies.
- On the **West Bank** and round Jerusalem, there were nearly 400,000 Jewish settlers and tens of thousands of troops. There were over 2 million Palestinians but the Israelis controlled over 70 per cent of the land and had complete control of the water and electricity supplies. The Israelis controlled the main roads and they restricted the movements of the Palestinians with checkpoints, road blocks and night-time **curfews**.

The Israelis seemed to be consolidating their hold on the land, and certainly not recognising any Palestinian claim to a national homeland. A more permanent peace and an independent Palestinian state seemed more distant than ever.

CLINTON'S FINAL BID FOR PEACE, 2000

The US President Bill Clinton tried to revive the peace process. He invited the Israeli and **PLO** leaders to Camp David in America. For days on end, the two sides were locked in discussion, with the Americans trying to steer the negotiations towards a peaceful outcome. But the obstacles proved too great. In particular, the issues of Jerusalem and of the right of Palestinian refugees to return to Israel could not be resolved. The talks ended with no significant progress achieved. Many in the West blamed Arafat, accusing him of rejecting a deal that would have given Gaza and most of the West Bank to the Palestinians. Others defended him: how could the PLO accept a peace deal that did not grant them East Jerusalem, which was mainly Arab, as their capital?

OPERATION DEFENSIVE SHIELD, MARCH 2002

Meanwhile, the death toll in the Middle East mounted. **HAMAS** and other **militant** Palestinian groups carried out bombings both inside Israel and also against Israeli troops and settlers in the occupied territories. In March 2002, after 29 Israelis were killed in a HAMAS suicide bombing, the Israeli Prime Minister, Ariel Sharon, launched 'Operation Defensive Shield'.

Israeli troops, using tanks, carried out raids inside Palestinian towns and refugee camps on the West Bank and Gaza. They also embarked on a policy of targeted assassinations, often using helicopter gunships. They set out to kill Palestinian militants in their homes or offices. They were often successful and hit their targets, but women and children, frequently family members, were also killed. Even schools and hospitals were sometimes hit. These buildings may have contained HAMAS members but then organisations like HAMAS ran schools and hospitals as well as carrying out military activities. Life in the occupied territories became worse and worse. Fresh water and food became more scarce and very few people had paid work.

- Israel's 1967 borders
- Separation barrier and planned border with Palestine
- Land that would be annexed
- Israeli settlements
- Palestinian land occupied by Israel since 1967

WEST BANK

Jericho

Jerusalem

ISRAEL

Bethlehem

Dead Sea

Hebron

0   15 km

*ull extent of Israel's security barrier.

ISRAEL'S SECURITY BARRIER

By May 2003, over 2,000 Palestinians and 760 Israelis had been killed since the Intifada started in 2000. As the violence continued, Israel started to build a barrier around the West Bank. In some places, it was an eight-metre high concrete wall, in other places it was just a fence. It was reinforced by troops, barbed wire and CCTV cameras. The wall was not built along the '**green line**' that marked the pre-1967 boundary between Israel and the occupied territories, but was further into the West Bank.

Israelis said the wall was temporary and purely defensive, to keep out the bombers, but its opponents claimed it took more land from the Palestinians. They pointed out that many West Bank Jewish settlements were on the Israeli side and that some Palestinian villages found themselves on the 'wrong side' also. In other words, the Israelis were creating 'facts on the ground' so that any future Palestinian state would not include all of the West Bank occupied by Israel in the 1967 War.

Questions

a Why has it been so difficult to achieve peace between Israel and the Palestinians since 1993? You should refer in your answer to:
  • the building of Jewish settlements
  • suicide bombings
  • the second Intifada
  • the building of the security barrier.

Write some notes to answer each of the following questions:
• What were the origins of the Second Intifada?
• What was Operation Defensive Shield?
• Why, and with what effects, did Israel build a security barrier?
• Why do you think so much land round Jerusalem was enclosed on the Israeli side?

barrier being built in 2003.

A cartoon from The Times, *March 2004. It follows the killing of HAMAS leader, Sheikh Ahmed Yassin, a paralysed man who had to use a wheelchair. In the tank is Israeli Prime Minister, Ariel Sharon.*

ROAD MAP TO PEACE, 2003

In April 2003, US President George W. Bush published what he called a 'road map' for peace between Israel and the Palestinians. His country was about to invade Iraq and topple the government of Saddam Hussein and he was keen to show that he was just as concerned about the Palestinian problem as he was about oil-rich Iraq. The road map outlined a step-by-step timetable towards a Palestinian state. The first phase was to depend on an end to Palestinian bombings, Israeli raids on Palestinian towns and settlement-building.

At first, the 'road map' made little difference. The Palestinian bombings continued and so did Israel's targeted assassinations. In March 2004, an Israeli helicopter missile killed the spiritual leader of HAMAS as he left a mosque near his home in Gaza. The cartoon above comments on this.

PEACE REVIVED, 2004–05

However, over the next two years, there were signs of the peace process being revived. In April 2004, the Israeli government announced that it would evacuate all Jewish settlers and troops from Gaza. In November 2004, Yasser Arafat died and was succeeded by Mahmoud Abbas who became Chairman of the PLO and was elected President of the Palestinian Authority. In February 2005, Abbas persuaded Palestinian militants to call a halt, even if only temporary, to their bombing. Then the Israeli and Palestinian leaders met in Egypt and announced a mutual ceasefire. In the summer of 2005, Jewish settlers and troops were withdrawn from Gaza.

Nevertheless, the issue of Jewish settlements on the West Bank remained a great obstacle to peace. This is shown in the sources that follow.

A SOURCE

Donald Macintyre reports from the West Bank (for the *Independent* newspaper), November 2004.

On the hilltop above us is the Jewish West Bank settlement. In the valley below is the Palestinian olive grove. Abu Adas looks up and says: 'the land of the settlement is the land of my grandfather. I could bear the loss if only they would let us pick our olives down here in the valley and live in peace. We live in constant fear of being shot at by the settlers, whose final goal is to terrorise us and drive us off the land.'

Today, however, the villagers can harvest their crop in relative safety because they have been joined by Jewish volunteers led by Arik Ascherman, the director of Rabbis for Human Rights, which has been campaigning for olive farmers to be allowed to harvest their crop in safety. Having won the confidence of the Palestinian farmers by rising at dawn day after day to pick olives side by side with them, Rabbi Ascherman provides a rare example of grassroots Jewish–Arab dialogue.

SOURCE

A Jewish rabbi, Arik Ascherman, leads a group of Jewish volunteers who help Palestinian villagers on the West Bank to harvest olives.

D SOURCE

'A Jewish Voice for Peace' is the name of a group of American Jews campaigning for peace between Israel and the Palestinians.

It is false to see the settlements as ordinary villages or towns where Israelis only want to live in peace with their Palestinian neighbours. They are in fact imposed by force – superior Israeli military force – on Palestinian territory. Many have been built precisely to assert Israeli power and ownership. They are not peaceful villages but militarised encampments.

C SOURCE

Donald Macintyre reports from the town of Hebron on the West Bank (for the *Independent* newspaper), March 2006.

Hebron is the second-largest Palestinian city on the West Bank but at its centre, near the site of a Jewish holy place, live 600 Jews who believe it is their God-given right to be there.

If Hebron was anything like a normal city, it would take Abu Heikel about three minutes to drive home from the coffee shop he runs in the main shopping area to his home. But like the other 35,000 Palestinians who live in the Israeli-controlled sector of Hebron, Abu Heikel isn't allowed to use a car. Instead he passes on foot through four Israeli Army checkpoints on his way home. The area used to be a commercial centre but today it is a ghost town. It is inhabited by just 600 Jewish settlers in four small settlements in the heart of the city.

There are no school buses for Abu Heikel's children; the only vehicles allowed in the Israeli-controlled sector are those of the settlers and the continuously patrolling Jeeps of the Israeli troops here to protect them – 1,500 in all, or just under three soldiers for every settler.

Questions

a Explain what Source A tells us about Jewish settlements on the West Bank.
b How useful is Source B to a historian studying Jewish attitudes towards settlements on the West Bank?
c Sources C and D give different views of the role of Israeli troops in Jewish settlements. Why do you think they are different?
d Do you agree that the continued building of Jewish settlements on Palestinian land proves that the Israelis do not really want peace? Give reasons.

Key Issue

- What are the challenges of peacemaking?

HAMAS VICTORY IN PALESTINIAN ELECTIONS, 2006

The Israeli–Palestinian conflict has continued to remain in the news. Even a Palestinian election in 2006 was a big news item. In that year, elections were held for the Palestinian parliament. All adult Palestinians on the West Bank and in Gaza were entitled to vote. Up until this time, most of the seats in the Parliament had been held by members of **Fatah**, which was the main body inside the **PLO**. Increasingly, however, ordinary Palestinians saw Fatah and many of the PLO leaders as corrupt and ineffective. There was widespread frustration, anger and bitterness about the poverty and squalor in which so many of them lived.

In the elections, **HAMAS** won the majority of seats. Mahmoud Abbas, a member of Fatah, remained as President of the Palestinian Authority and maintained his contacts with members of the Israeli government but the HAMAS majority in the Palestinian Parliament refused to recognise the state of Israel. As a result, Israel, the USA and most European governments refused to have any dealings with HAMAS. The peace process stalled yet again.

WAR IN LEBANON, JULY 2006

In July 2006, fighters belonging to **Hizbollah**, a **militant** Lebanese organisation, crossed the border into Israel and captured two Israeli soldiers. They then demanded the release of hundreds of Hizbollah fighters and Palestinians who were held in Israeli jails. Israel refused to agree to a swap and launched air attacks on Hizbollah strongholds, both in south Lebanon and Beirut, the capital. Hizbollah hit back. They launched hundreds of missiles, from the south of Lebanon, against towns in the north of Israel.

Israeli planes bombed Beirut airport and bridges leading to Syria which they believed to be the source of Hizbollah missiles. Within a month, the death toll in Lebanon reached a thousand, mostly civilians, with nearly a million made homeless. Nearly a hundred Israelis were killed. In August 2006, a ceasefire was arranged at the **United Nations** and fighting stopped. A UN peacekeeping force was sent to the Israeli–Lebanese border.

Palestinian refugee children in Beirut, Lebanon, 1996. Now adults, these children have still not known peace.

PROSPECTS FOR ISRAELI–PALESTINIAN PEACE

The heart of the conflict in the Middle East still remains the Palestinian problem. The real test of peacemaking will be the success that both Israeli and Palestinian leaders have in controlling their **extremists** and keeping the support of the majority of their people. On both sides there will always be extremists and those who oppose any compromise. On the Israeli side are those who believe that the West Bank must remain in Israeli hands because it is the 'promised land' that God gave to the Jews. On the Palestinian side are those who still believe that all of Palestine must be restored to the Palestinians, even if it means the destruction of Israel.

After nearly 60 years of war, millions of Israelis and Palestinians want peace. The economies of both the Israelis and the Palestinians are devastated by violence. Israel knows that about 200,000 of its citizens are emigrating each year (mostly to the USA) and that, the longer the violence continues, the more this number will increase. Meanwhile, the Palestinian population grows. This may be one reason why the Israelis have built the Wall, their security barrier; many Israelis are happy for the Palestinians to have a state of their own as long as they are enclosed. But a settlement dictated by one side will not bring lasting peace.

The main issues remain the same as ever: the borders of any Palestinian state, the Jewish **settlements** on the West Bank, the future of Jerusalem and the Palestinian **refugees**' right to return. Both sides have more to gain from negotiating, from discussing and deciding how to make peace. It will require great courage from their leaders.

Syria will also have to be brought into the peace process. Unlike Egypt and Jordan, she has never made a peace treaty with Israel. She has still not regained the Golan Heights which Israel captured in 1967.

Above all, peacemaking will require the whole-hearted support of the American government. The USA is the one country that can put enough pressure on Israel to reach a negotiated settlement with the Palestinians and, at the same time, assure the Jewish state of its protection. The USA supplies Israel with over $3 billion of aid every year as well as the most advanced military equipment. Therefore it has huge influence in peacemaking.

Only when peace between Israel and the Palestinians is secure will the threat from terrorism, both in the Middle East and the world as a whole, be reduced.

Questions

a Give one reason why Israeli, American and many European governments refused to have any dealings with HAMAS.

b What effect is continuing violence having on the Israeli population?

c Why does the USA have such an important role in making peace between Israel and the Palestinians?

The Palestinian town of Bethlehem. Can this West Bank town, birthplace of Jesus, become a symbol of peace again?

GLOSSARY

anti-Semitism – actions or feelings of hatred against the Jews

blockade – the blocking of a place by troops or ships to prevent goods reaching it

civil war – a war between people of the same country

Cold War – the state of tension (but not actual war) which existed between the USSR and the USA from the late 1940s to the late 1980s

curfew – a time or signal for people to remain indoors

extremist – a person who has very strong opinions or aims which he or she refuses to change in any circumstances

Fatah – a Palestinian organisation which carried out raids against Israel

fedayeen – men trained to carry out raids (literally, those who sacrifice themselves)

'green line' – the border between Israel and the West Bank before the Six-Day War of 1967

guerrilla – a soldier who avoids fighting in open battle when possible; he prefers to use tactics like ambushes and hit-and-run raids

Haganah – a Jewish defence force set up in the 1920s

HAMAS – a radical Palestinian organisation

Holocaust – the mass murder of the Jews in the Second World War

Hizbollah – an Islamic group based in South Lebanon

immigration – the arrival of people to settle in a new country

Intifada – the Palestinian uprising in the West Bank and Gaza

Irgun – a small, secret Jewish organisation which fought for Jewish independence

kibbutzim – settlements in Israel where people live and work together

League of Nations – the international organisation founded, after the end of the First World War, to keep the peace

mandate – power given to a country to look after another country

martyrs – people who sacrifice themselves for a cause

militant – person who supports the use of force

military service – the requirement to serve in the armed forces

mobilise – getting an army ready to fight

nationalise – the government taking over ownership of a company, industry or land

occupied territories – lands controlled by the troops of a foreign power (e.g. the West Bank and Gaza, occupied by the Israelis)

partition – division into two or more parts

persecute – to punish or treat cruelly, often because of religion or race

PLO – Palestine Liberation Organisation

propaganda – persuading people to believe certain ideas and behave in a certain way; sometimes involves telling lies

refugees – people forced to leave their home by war or natural disaster

reprisal – an action against an enemy to stop him from doing something again

reservists – people who could be called up to serve in the armed forces

retaliate – to hit back

settlement – a group of houses (e.g. as built by the Israelis on the West Bank and in Gaza)

superpowers – the two biggest powers, the USA and USSR, after the Second World War

synagogue – a building where Jews worship

United Nations – the international organisation, established at the end of the Second World War, to keep the peace

UNRWA – United Nations Relief and Works Agency, which was set up to run the refugee camps

USSR – the Union of Soviet Socialist Republics, the official name for communist Russia from 1917 to 1991. Also known as the Soviet Union.

Yom Kippur – (Day of Atonement) an important Jewish religious day of fasting and annual Jewish holiday

Zionist – someone who believed that the Jews should have a national homeland and, later, an independent state.

Although every effort has been made to ensure that website addresses are correct at time of going to press, Hodder Murray cannot be held responsible for the content of any website mentioned in this book. It is sometimes possible to find a relocated web page by typing in the address of the home page for a website in the URL window of your browser.

Hachette UK's policy is to use papers that are natural, renewable and recyclable products and made from wood grown in sustainable forests. The logging and manufacturing processes are expected to conform to the environmental regulations of the country of origin.

Orders: please contact Bookpoint Ltd, 130 Milton Park, Abingdon, Oxon OX14 4SB. Telephone: (44) 01235 827720. Fax: (44) 01235 400454. Lines are open 9.00 – 5.00, Monday to Saturday, with a 24-hour message answering service. Visit our website at www.hoddereducation.co.uk

© Michael Scott-Baumann 1998
First published in 1998 by
Hodder Education,
an Hachette UK company,
338 Euston Road
London NW1 3BH

Second edition published in 2007

Impression number   10 9 8
Year   2015 2014 2013

Cover illustration by David Angel
Illustrations by Tony Jones at Art Construction
Typeset in 10.5/12pt Berling Roman by Fakenham Prepress Solutions
Printed in Dubai

A catalogue record for this title is available from the British Library

ISBN 978 0340 929 346